General
Hermann Göring

Prime Minister of Prussia

Germany Reborn

First Edition - March 1934
Reprinted - March 1934

OCR - Edition
LENCULUS
Exegi monumentum aere perennius
March 2018

Contents

Foreword
Introduction
1. Germany's Heritage .14
2. The War .18
3. The Rebellion .21
4. Versailles .26
5. Weimar .29
6. Finis Germaniae ? .34
7. Adolf Hitler .38
8. Black Friday - November 9, 1923 .44
9. The Tactics of Legality .28
10. The Leader .53
11. The Brüning Government .60
12. The Papen Government .66
13. The Schleicher Government .69
14. The Victory - January 30, 1933 .73
15. My Task .78
   (a) The Reorganization of the Police
   (b) The Organization of the State Secret Police
   (c) The wiping out of Marxism and Communism
   (d) Prime Minister of Prussia
   (e) Aviation
16. The Making of a Nation .91
17. For Equal Rights, Honour and Peace .95

Foreword

I welcome this opportunity of presenting to the English-speaking peoples a few of my ideas about the struggle of the German people for freedom and honour. I hope that these words will also be accepted by our opponents as a frank expression of my boundless love for my country, to whose service alone I have pledged my whole life.

Hermann Göring

Berlin, February, 1934.

Introduction

At the time Third Reich German Nazi leader Hermann Göring wrote the following manuscript, he was still a general. Later, Hermann Göring became a Reichsmarschall (Reich Marshal).

In World One War, Hermann Göring took over command of von Richthofen's squadron after the Red Baron was shot down. Soon after the war Hermann Göring became a follower of Adolf Hitler. After the failed "Putsch", he fled to Sweden and got married. For a while he stayed in Italy, but the ruling fascists had little to gain from helping the then banned NSDAP. But when Hitler was released from Spandau prison, Hermann Göring was soon at his side again.

Hermann Göring was intensely involved in the political fraction negotiations. Late in the Weimar Republik Hermann Göring even become President of the Reichstag.

After the NSDAP took power, Hermann Göring became Minister President of Prussia. Hermann Göring's re-organization of the Prussian police is described in the manuscript on this page. Already a top Nazi leader, Hermann Göring became a top level Third Reich leader well, both in politics and as head of the new and rapidly expanding Luftwaffe - which eventually even had its own tank formation, the Hermann Göring Panzer Division !
When Hermann Göring re-married (his first wife had died), the wedding was one of the biggest social events in the Third Reich.

When the Second War World broke out, Germany had the best - but not the largest - air force in the world. It lost this lead during the war, but near the end regained it with the ME262 jet. Many experts believe Germany might have won the war, if it could have held out another six months, ie enough time to build ENOUGH jets to turn the tide in the air.

Hermann Göring had received a very painful wound in the groin. This medication eventually led to a drug addiction, which in turn had a negative effect on his work. Hermann Göring liked to be generous to his friends, for which he has been criticized.

Despite Hermann Göring's shortcomings, Hitler remained loyal to his friend and comrade until very late in the war when Hermann Göring attempted to negotiate peace with the west without Hitler's permission.

At Nuremberg Field Marshal Hermann Göring put up a spirited fight. In the end, Hermann Göring defied the enemy's desire to hang him by claiming suicide.

1. Germany's Heritage

Germany's Heritage

The lack of understanding and sympathy which many foreign peoples show for Germany is very largely due to ignorance of the special and peculiar character of German history.

'Human history is the history of war,' and the history of the German people is also a long tale of cruel wars : 'From the battle against Ariovistus to the struggle of the unarmed on the Ruhr an iron chain stretches' (Stegemann). Since the idea of Germany and a German people has been known in history, we see that the bond which it implies has been only the bond of blood and of common culture and a common language. Now and then the loose conglomerate has seemed to take on a firmer form, but right down to modern times it has never coalesced to form a German Nation. This is one of the reasons why the German people as a whole has never taken part in great wars of conquest. Usually the different parts of Germany have fought against each other, very often to the advantage of other peoples. But for centuries the Germans were compelled to defend their own homes and their own land - the land first of their tribe and finally of the people. Germany possesses no natural boundaries. It was never a castle whose fortifications were sea and mountains, but lay like an open camp in the midst of Europe, protected only by the bodies of its men. And that is also the reason why the Germans never fought their wars for foreign crowns, but always for their own honour; not to conquer foreign countries, but to defend their own freedom; not to subdue others, but to ensure their own security.

The arduous path of the German people through their history begins with the partition of the German Empire by the Treaty of Verdun in the year 843 and leads past the 'Testament of Richelieu' and the Peace of Westphalia, which claimed to have assured for ever the 'Libertés germaniques,' to the Dictate of Versailles in the year 1919.

These 'German Freedoms' meant nothing less than the perpetual partition of the Reich into countless little kingdoms and principalities, which were played off against one another by the neighbouring countries, according to Louis XI's principle 'Divide et impera.'

And then at last Prussia took over its great mission in world history. That was - to fight for the unity of the German Reich. That was a task formidable enough for that incomparable genius, Frederick II. Even his enemies called him 'the Great.' He was at once 'the most kingly of men and the most human of kings.' In a life of unexampled austerity he made of little Prussia the foundation of the coming Reich. As he lay on the simple camp-bed that had seen so many campaigns, and alone in the arms of his hussar breathed his last breath, his last words remained as a Testament to his successors, 'I see the promised land from afar, but I shall not set foot in it.'

After Frederick the Great came the Reichsfreiherr vom Stein who fought passionately for his great ideal : 'I know only one Fatherland - and that is called Germany !' But he, too, after a valiant life of work, battles and defeats, the victim of slander and treachery, could only win a partial victory. He, too, knew of the coming unity, but was not to experience it.

After Stein - Bismarck. Born on an estate in the Mark Brandenburg, he continued and almost completed the gigantic task begun by Frederick and Stein. But Bismarck at the moment of death, as if death itself had torn a veil from his eyes, cried, full of sorrow and misgiving, these last words - 'Germany - Germany'.

Under the flags in the Hall of Mirrors at Versailles, in which Bismarck's Reich was born, stood Lieutenant von Hindenburg. He had fought on the battlefield of Königgrätz and in the war against France. In the greatest of all wars his imperial master called him to the head of the mighty army which for four years withstood a hostile world.

Somewhere in this vast bulwark of German men, there stood one who, unknown like the countless others, and brave as so many others were brave, was destined to write his name in the eternal book of History as the saviour of the German people, the man who was to consummate her solidarity and unity. That man was Adolf Hitler.

In the three great wars won by Prussia in the last century, Germany was born : on the battlefields of Leipzig and Waterloo, of Königgrätz and Sedan, men of German blood found each other again. Before the guns of Paris and in the palace of Louis XIV the age-old German dream of a German Empire was fulfilled. Through the concentration of all national forces an unprecedented advance took place. A peace of nearly 50 years under the protection of a strong army and a good fleet enabled the young Reich brilliantly to build up its industry and ensure prosperity. Whereas the population of Germany in 1871 was 41 millions, in 1914 it had risen to nearly 70 millions. A vast host of human beings was pressing onward, was working in fields and factories, in laboratories and mines, behind counters and desks or in harbours and wharves all over the world. This great success is known to the world and can be statistically demonstrated.

Germany was first in the markets of the world as regards electrical apparatus, the glass and toy industry, and smelting and mining. The German chemical industry alone supplied four-fifths of the world market. German trade with harbours outside Europe had increased 500 per cent up to the beginning of the century. Thus Germany, in peaceful competition, by hard work, efficiency and organization, had grown to be a mighty factor in the economic life of the world. This position, won through peaceful work, led finally to the most terrible of all conflicts, the World War. The encirclement of Germany was complete, and the peoples of Europe plunged into a sea of blood and misery, and the whole world into a catastrophe of incalculable extent.

On the 28th June, 1914, a 19-year-old student in Sarajevo shot the Austrian heir apparent. This shot suddenly and pitilessly let loose the thunderstorm which had been brooding over Europe for years. The first rumblings were produced by the never ending railway trains which brought the already mobilized Russian army corps to the German frontier. The gigantic engine of war began its deadly pounding. Europe was mobilizing!

The die had been cast. Threatened from all sides, Germany had the sword thrust into her hand. The German people, guiltless of the outbreak of this greatest of wars, had to fight in order to defend their life and honour.

2. The War

The most precious possession that a people can have, its 'freedom and honour,' was threatened. And the German people did its duty. The German army, in order that it should not itself be overthrown and destroyed, march through Belgium. It was self-defence in the highest sense of the word. It is true that the peoples of the different countries, whether of Germany or of England, of France or Russia, felt themselves to be guiltless. They obeyed their governments and did their duty. The German people too, from Emperor to peasant, from Field Marshal to private, were deeply convinced of their own innocence and believed unflinchingly in the justice of their cause. For four long years the German soldier fought heroically and chivalrously.

The army and the people suffered grievously from the terrible enemy propaganda concerning so-called atrocities. It may be that our enemies honestly believed that it was necessary to use such Propaganda in order to alienate the sympathies of the world from the brave German people. It may be that they really believed that faked evidence and faked Photos were necessary to this end. Germany knew that all this was simply calumny. To be sure, war is hard. The fate of the individual becomes insignificant over against the fate of whole nations, but it was never the German way to torment and discredit their enemies. Love of cruelty was never part of the Germanic character. Many a French or Belgian child, who had lost a hand or arm or leg which, according to the Photos, had been hacked off by the Germans, could now reveal that these mutilations were caused by the shells or bombs of their own countrymen. Such things are unavoidable in war. I myself fought on the Western Front from the first day of the War to the last, and can state on my word of honour that the German soldiers always endeavoured to ease the hard lot of the civil Population.

Never has any people in the history of the world had to hold its own in such a mighty struggle as the German people were compelled to do during these years. No epic could describe what heroism, what patient endurance, what devotion to duty were shown on all fronts. For four years the German army held at bay a world of enemies, vastly superior in numbers and war material, and defended their country from invasion. For four years the

German people endured and suffered grievously as in a besieged city. Every man who was capable of bearing arms, old men and boys, went out to join in the deadly struggle. And at home German women by their Patient endurance and forgetfulness of self proved their greatness and nobility. In spite of all of the enemy's efforts Germany seemed unconquerable. But at last came the bitter end, the terrible defeat.

After long years, during which the blood of the best men had been spilt, after long years of hunger and attrition, a Party consisting of traitors to their country succeeded in confusing the people at home and in poisoning its soul. Supported by enemy propaganda, bribed with the enemy's money, Social Democrat agitators stirred up the people. Germany, bleeding from a thousand wounds, starving and exhausted, heroically carried on the fight against the enemies from without, but she was no longer strong enough to withstand the enemy within. The people was stirred up against its leaders with the slogan 'For the freedom of your class ! For the freedom of the individual !' Strikes in munitions works were organized by Social Democrat leaders, and the same leaders drew up appeals to commit treachery or to desert. And so at last the fate of the army - which was still fighting bravely - was sealed. This bravest of all armies had its backbone broken from behind. What the enemy would never have been able to do in open battle they achieved through their alliance with the German Social Democrats; but, in spite of all, the troops unconquered carried back their unspotted shield of honour, and their victorious banners.

The mightiest struggle of history was at an end. Germany had lost the War and her freedom, but her enemies were only in appearance the victors.

The countries of the west were on the verge of collapse, and Europe threatened to disappear in chaos.

# 3. The Rebellion

With the disastrous end of the War the German people began its time of trial. With the introduction of pernicious doctrines of the Jew Karl Marx into Germany began the attack on the strength of the Reich and the attempt to undermine the peace and wellbeing of the people. The basis of Marxism is class war, and the destruction of national unity is its point of departure. German is set against German; the enemy is no longer the adversary beyond the frontier, but only those fellow-countrymen within who belong to a different social stratum. If Marxism was to succeed, a strong and contented Germany had to be made weak and discontented. And so for many decades Marxists were working systematically with this end in view. Everywhere hatred, envy, discontent and suspicion were being preached and the stability of the Reich was being undermined. Now the Army and Navy have always symbolized the strength of a people. It was therefore against the armed forces of the State that Marxism directed its passionate hatred.
And so, wherever it could, the Social Democratic party injured the prestige of the army, refused to vote for supplies, and undermined discipline.

For decades this party carried on an agitation against all authority, undermined existing institutions by every means, in order finally, with one last stab in the back, to overthrow the State itself. It was a matter of indifference to this party that Germany herself, by losing the War, would be given over to destruction.

And so on the 9th November, 1918, that vile rising of mutineers took place and Marxist dominance was established. On the same day there began for the poor tormented German people that period of history that may be described as 'The Period of German Shame and Tribulation.' From the steps of the Reichstag, Scheidemann, a prominent leader of the Social Democrats, proclaimed "Today the German people are victorious all along the line." And at that very moment the German people plunged from proud heights into the abyss. It was not the people which was 'victorious' on that day, for all the best elements of the people still stood on all fronts, ready to give their last drop of blood in defence of their country.

Only those traitors were victorious for whom the very idea of a Fatherland was non-existent. Those cowards who had deserted from the front were victorious, that human scum that always makes its appearance in times of stress. It was Marxism that was victorious. But wherever Marxism is victorious, at that same moment a nation collapses. Where Communism raises its head a people is destroyed.

The returning soldiers, without leaders, uprooted from their civil occupations, estranged from their homes, disappointed and even desperate, fell an easy prey to Marxist agitation. Social Democracy increased enormously, took over the leadership everywhere and from that time on became responsible for Germany's destiny. An unspeakable hatred was preached against everything which did not conform to Marxist doctrine. The brilliant past was trod in the dust, and scorn and ridicule were heaped on everything which the people still held sacred. Morality was banished and immorality was declared moral. The very idea of patriotism was denounced and national Parties were destroyed. For the strength and power which lies in national unity was to be substituted international solidarity. The class-conscious proletarian was to take the place of the patriotic German. Germany broke up into two camps, on the one side the Proletariat, on the other the Bourgeoisie. The whole German people had to atone terribly for this crime of class war.

But in accusing Social Democracy of this crime of treason towards the people, one must not forget that it was made possible only because the Middle Classes altogether failed to act.

The Middle Class had even before the War degenerated to become the Bourgeoisie. The complete bankruptcy of Middle Class leadership before the War, the lack of understanding on the part of the Middle Classes for the German worker, their snobbery and self-conceit, made it possible that the leaderless German worker should prove all too susceptible to the seductions of Marxism and should lend a ready ear to demagogues who were mostly of an alien race and who claimed to represent the interests of the working class.

If one looks back at the time before the War, one is amazed to see how weak the leaders of the nation really were and with what apathy they looked on while the people were being duped.

But one will also be amazed to see what a high percentage of the Social Democratic leaders and agitators were Jews. But now in the days of the post-War rising these Jewish leaders sprouted from the ground like poisonous fungi. Wherever soldiers' councils were formed Jews were the leaders, those very same Jews who had not been seen out at the front, but had been employed in the supply departments at the base or had filled indispensable official and military posts at home. In the streets the mob raged. Soldiers had their badges and shoulder-straps torn off. The flag, which for decades had symbolized the greatness of the Reich, was trampled in the mud. On all buildings fluttered the red flag of rebellion; everywhere there was disorder and dissolution. This disorder was deliberately displayed in the way people deported themselves, to make it quite clear that now everyone could do, or not do, what he liked. There was to be no State, no order, no authority, and the moral conception of freedom was to be rejected in favour of immoral shamelessness. The misled soldiers began slowly to sink to the level of a mere rabble. Dissolution grew daily, even hourly; radicals had their places taken by even more extreme radicals; and gradually it seemed as if the new rulers, who had set themselves at the head of the nation with such high-sounding proclamations, would themselves be drawn into the whirlpool of destruction. They could no longer get rid of the spirits they had invoked. The independent Social Democrats pressed forward, and then these too were overtaken and were succeeded by the Spartacists. In this chaos, which the new leaders could do nothing to overcome, there was only one way out. An appeal was made to the remnants of the army, once so powerful, but now so weak.

In the midst of the general dissolution, a few thousand who were not willing timidly to abandon everything, had come together in order to withstand the general collapse and to defend their ideals of patriotism and honour. These were the Volunteer Corps, and to them the new Government appealed. They were cleverly able to befool the Volunteer Corps into believing that they would have to come forward to save their country, by which the leaders of the Government really meant their own power and safety. The unpolitical soldiers of the Volunteer Corps did not understand the true state of things. They were accustomed always to intervene where their country was in danger, and so once more without thinking of themselves they did their duty. They staked their lives and threw themselves into the battle against the Spartacist rabble. But hardly had they won and become masters of the situation and hardly did the Government feel itself safe in the saddle, when it showed its true face and rewarded the Volunteer Corps by dissolving them and throwing them on to the streets.

But to the world the German Social Democrats suddenly proclaimed themselves to be the maintainers of order, the guardians of the Reich. Even today one still frequently hears the objection that the Social Democrats did at any rate in 1918 and 1919 save the Reich by courageously restoring order. Ebert, Schneidemann and Noske are said to have saved the Reich from dissolution. With the Social Democrats we are accustomed to such distortions of fact and such attempts to divest themselves of responsibility. The delegates of the people had announced in high-sounding proclamations that the age of freedom had dawned, that the worker was now ruler in the land and that he would have little work and large earnings, that the age of peace and universal prosperity was at hand, that the other nations would joyfully welcome a Germany (freed from militarism and monarchic tyranny), that poverty and want would cease, that corruption would be abolished; in short, that the Golden Age was about to begin. But they forgot that before this famous proclamation the German people did not even know what corruption meant.

It was left to the Social Democrats to introduce corruption as one of the most essential phenomena of their rule. The end of the proclamation was that Germany was now to become a land of freedom, beauty and honour. None of these promises, not one of them, was kept. On the contrary, one can today show conclusively that the exact opposite took place.

4. Versailles

The dream was abruptly dispelled and so was the hope of eternal peace, of future happiness and of the prosperity of all peoples. Suddenly, into the midst of this joyful music of the future, into the midst of this drivel about humanity, there sounded sharply and discordantly the trumpets of Versailles. For the first time Germany awoke from the intoxication of civil strife. In a flash it was seen that Germany had again been deceived. Trusting in Wilson's words and in his Fourteen Points, the sword had been laid aside. Germany had trustfully abandoned herself to the assurances concerning the universal happiness of peoples and international solidarity. And now she saw herself defenceless against a world bristling with armaments and hatred. 'Germaniam esse delendam' was the slogan of Versailles. More devilish than the mind of a Dante could have imagined, were the Peace terms of Versailles. Never has any people in the history of the world been presented with such terms. Even the destruction of Carthage was as nothing compared to the shameful Peace of Versailles. The word Peace seemed shamed and desecrated for ever. A brave people, peaceful and hard-working, loving freedom and honour, was now confined in the prisonhouse of Versailles. The thirst for revenge was now satisfied by the destruction of the once feared, but also respected, enemy. In their blind hatred the enemies of Germany did not see that, with this so-called Peace, they were leading, not only Germany, but the whole world to catastrophe.

But in Germany the Marxist angels of peace continued, in spite of everything, to prate before the people of international solidarity. The blame for the Dictate of Versailles was put down to having lost the War, but it was forgotten that the Social Democrats themselves had made the collapse of the German people possible through their treacherous action. But the German people realized too late that it had in the past months thrown away its honour, and that now, without honour, it was deprived of its freedom as well. Only once did it rise again as one man when the shame became unbearable; the German generals were to be delivered up ! What Englishman, what Frenchman would not blush with shame if such a suggestion were made to his people ?

But we Germans know today that our enemies would never have made such humiliating demands if they had not seen Germany's moral collapse before them. Only because they had seen how the German leaders at that time were destroying every idea of honour and national pride, could inflict such humiliations on Germany.

5. Weimar

The Marxist-Democratic National Assembly of Weimar was nevertheless not ashamed to make the Versailles Treaty the foundation of the new German constitution. The Weimar state was born of treachery and cowardice, its corner-stones were misery and shame. The new Germany, however, received the full blessings of this democracy in the form of uncontrolled parliamentarianism. All ideas were turned upside down. The distinguishing mark of parliamentarianism, in contrast to the principle of leadership, is that authority is given from below upwards and responsibility from above downwards. That is to say, innumerable parties and their delegates impose their authority on the government and the government has to obey them. The government is therefore responsible to these parties and is the plaything of their interests. But the laws of Nature demand that authority should be exercised from above downwards and responsibility from below upwards. Each leader has authority and he issues his orders to officials and followers below him. But he is responsible only to his superiors, and the leader at the top is responsible to the people as a whole and to their future. In the past it has only been by virtue of this principle that anything has been achieved; only by this principle could nations arise and history be made. But in Germany, Parliament now ruled, the anonymous idea of the Majority ruled, the cowardice of mere members was the dominant factor.

In the midst of these divisions of class and party, countless groups sought their own advantage at the expense of the people. Marxism celebrated its greatest triumphs. The princes had been driven away and the red masters climbed into the vacant thrones, but did not on that account become rulers. Above them all the Golden Calf was enthroned and the parties continued their grotesque dance, In every walk of life we see decadence and decay, the breakup of the Nation grows yearly more apparent, and the Reich is, from now on, a shadow, a framework held together with difficulty, already brittle in many places and without any sense or purpose. Corruption, immorality and indecency were the outward signs of the 'proud' Republic. And the decline of culture begins with the loosening of morals.

And then came the terrible inflation. Since the attempt had been made, in proper Marxist fashion, to destroy all cultural, ideal and moral values, it was only logical that this campaign of destruction should now be directed against the economic life of the nation. Marxism can thrive only when there are people who are discontented, homeless, uprooted from the soil and therefore receptive to false doctrines. The attempt was made to create in every social stratum a proletariat. The German was to be made, morally and materially, a proletarian. Thus the inflation destroyed any prosperity that still remained.

Wherever there was inherited property it was destroyed. Thousands were plunged into poverty overnight. The last remnants of property were destroyed by the inflation and by a purely Bolshevist system of taxation. One has only to think of that Witches' Sabbath of soaring millions. Was this the economic programme of Marxism ? Was this what they meant by complete socialization ? Later they modestly called the inflation a natural phenomenon and forgot that it was only the result of their criminal doctrines. Here again we see the close connection which ultimately exists between Marxism and Liberalism.

How could the Bourgeoisie be surprised when the poorest sections of the population now suddenly applied to the economic sphere the ideas of equality, freedom and fraternity preached in the name of Liberalism ? One could see at once how the boundaries between Social Democracy and the Middle Class parties became ever less distinct. The Social Democrat leaders became more and more bourgeois and sought to defend and keep what they had gained, for their own personal profit. Their slogan was no longer 'To the Barricades !' They were suddenly for law and order. On the other hand, the Middle Class parties contributed to the general collapse by their lack of character.

Today we accuse Social Democracy - whether, as at the beginning, in its red Jacobite cap, or, as later, in top hat - of having cheated and robbed Germany; but we must not forget that the Bourgeois parties, and above all the eternally vacillating Centre Party, participated in this wherever it occurred.

In spite of all philosophical differences between the Black and the Red parties, the Black never left the Red in the lurch. Parties ruled, unrestrained and unchecked, through parliament, but weary and heavy-laden the people had to bear their cross of suffering.

Together with this inner dissolution, Germany's prestige abroad suffered more and more. All love of country having been proscribed and all manly virtues derided, it was only logical that the German government should be condemned to complete impotence in its foreign policy. Germany had become the whipping-boy of international politics. Conflicting interests between the other Powers were settled at Germany's expense. The League of Nations seemed to be exclusively an instrument to keep Germany down and to protect the Treaty of Versailles. In accordance with the terms of that Treaty, Germany had completely disarmed and had thus become completely defenceless. With a zeal which was worthy of a nobler cause the German Governments had supervised and carried out this disarmament. But they went even further than the Treaty of Versailles required. They disarmed the German people morally and spiritually as well. They killed all will to live and to resist. In the insane desire for fulfilment of' all the provisions of the Treaty they became intoxicated with astronomical figures. Since they had robbed the people of their honour they were dishonourable themselves towards friend and foe. In place of a straightforward, honest and dignified policy which would be practicable even in times of the greatest disaster, they carried out a policy of trickery. They tried to get round the most difficult problems of foreign policy by appealing to international solidarity. It was altogether characteristic of German parliamentary policy not to solve problems but to escape from every vital question by means of some cowardly compromise.

And then came Communism. it developed inevitably from the false doctrines of Marxism. Communism raised its head as an inevitable result of a policy of cowardice and self-surrender, and, encouraged by a policy alternating between Marxist trickery and Middle Class cowardice, it was inevitably victorious. At the birth of the Republic there were only a few thousand followers of

Communism; but after a few years the number had risen to six millions, and Communism was prepared to seize power and to destroy culture, morals, the church and industry. It was ready to plunge Germany into chaos. Poverty and despair had seized the German people and driven them in their thousands into the arms of Communism. Millions of men, filled with hatred, wished to destroy, because everything in them had been destroyed, and there were leaders ready for these desperate, deluded people. These leaders came from the underworld and were the scum of the population.

And here, too, the Jew was more strongly represented than elsewhere. With the sub-man's will to destroy he felt that his time had come. The flag was hoisted. Blood red it fluttered, with the star of the Soviets in the middle. If this symbol should conquer, then Germany must go under in a rising flood of Bolshevism.

6. Finis Germaniae ?

Germany seemed lost. How was it possible that a people which had just fought such a heroic battle should fail so completely ? Was there no one ready to oppose the forces of destruction ? Somewhere there must still be bearers of the national honour. And there still were ! Right from the beginning resistance rallied. Everywhere war veterans got together, formed societies and organizations. They fought in the Volunteer Corps against the Spartacists and in Upper Silesia and on the Ruhr; they fought to overthrow the first great rising of the Communists, and freed Munich from the rule of the Workers' Councils. After they had been dissolved by the Government new organizations arose. Seldte founded in Magdeburg the Steel Helmets, the League of War Veterans. In Bavaria an Inhabitants' Defence Force was formed, and in the Alps the Oberland Corps. But each one was for itself.

There was no connection between them and they had at first only one aim, to restore law and order. But in the long run that could be no proper battle-cry, for Law and Order was, after all, what the well- fed Social Democrat bigwigs wanted themselves. To be sure, all these associations were filled with a passionate love of country and with a disgust for the prevailing system. But they lacked a firm basis, a really big aim, a bold plan of campaign. They were all filled with the great traditions of the past and were ready to defend them. But they were not the standard-bearers of a new future. Nevertheless we are deeply indebted to thein because they did not fail in the time of greatest need.

They became the rallying point for all who were prepared to fight for their country. But they would never have been able to overthrow the November State, because at the head of that State there were men who represented an idea, even though that idea was a destructive one. And one can never destroy an idea by force alone.

An idea can be overthrown only by substituting for it a new idea, which must be better and more convincing and whose representatives are filled with passionate energy. And a negative idea can be replaced only by a positive idea.

Ideas are eternal; they hang in the stars, and a man must be brave and strong enough to reach up to the stars and fetch down the fire from heaven and to carry the torch among men. In world history such men have always been the great prophets and often, too, the leaders of their people.

But where in Germany was the man who had both the genius and the strength to save his people and country ? The people looked in vain to those who by birth, education or the possession of material wealth or great names, were destined for leadership. But their greatness was past; these men did not put up the smallest resistance; they abandoned without a struggle what their ancestors had won throughout the centuries. Fate never forgives the man who abandons without a struggle what a benevolent providence has put into his hands. 'What you have inherited from your forefathers you must win anew in order to keep it.' This eternal truth was unfortunately ignored by the princely families of Germany. They were not prepared to risk anything, and had therefore no right to be surprised when others, too, did nothing for them and their possessions.

The aim of these princely houses was to retain certain material possessions, and for that aim they set their legal advisers to work. But the people, and above all the war veterans, saw amazed, in bitterness or despair, how those who were leaders by birth failed them. It was as a monarchist that I protested against the allegation that the monarchy was destroyed by the revolt of November 1918. The monarchist idea died in the German people in the course of the last fifteen years because the representatives of the monarchy had themselves dug its grave. In 1918, at the least opposition from the mob, they hauled down their once glorious standards, and in the same way they were not to be found in the ranks of those warriors who were passionately fighting for Germany's rebirth. There were a few notable exceptions, such as Prince August Wilhelm of Prussia, the family of the Landgraves of Hesse, Prince Waldeck, the Duke of Coburg, etc. But among the generals, too, there was not one who was willing to hoist the standard of resistance and to call upon all honourable war veterans to join in the fight against the system of shame and disgrace.

However splendidly German officers had fought in the War and however brilliant German generalship may have been, nevertheless the lack of political understanding which was characteristic of the German officer now had its bitter and fatal result. But the Middle Classes, even before the War, had not been able to produce any leaders. The possessing classes were at the best ready to represent their own personal interests, but not the interests of the German people as a whole.

7. Adolf Hitler

But when the need was greatest God gave the German people a champion, an unknown soldier of the World War, a man from the people, without rank or possessions or connections, a plain, simple man, but one who had overwhelming genius and greatness of character. A man of the people, Adolf Hitler arose and took German destiny into his clean strong hands and as the herald of German freedom and justice passed through all Germany, appealing, stirring up the people and inflaming their hearts like the incarnation of the German conscience itself. And then for all ardent, expectant Germans it seemed as if the beacon of the hidden Germany had lit up the starless night of hopeless despair. The German heart was found again, and with magic power it drew into itself the noblest blood and poured it out again into the people in countless streams of will and strength. The taskmasters of enslaved Germany might throw the 'rebels' into prison, might banish them, persecute, humiliate and insult them-but at no time could they force them to their knees. In hundreds thousands, tens and hundreds of thousands of hearts was the sacred seed of the German will to freedom sown. From farm to farm, from village to village, from the mountains to the sea, from the Rhine to beyond the Vistula, the flames of rebellion spread, rebellion against any and every kind of slavery. The flames at last became a vast sea of fire from which a purged and purified Germany arose to its divinely-appointed rank. 'For God does not wish that there should be slaves.'

Adolf Hitler knew that only as the standard-bearer of a new, a greater, a creative idea could his movement conquer, and so he gave it the philosophy of National Socialism, whose sacred symbol now floats victorious over a wonderfully united Germany.

The struggle for the new Germany could not be carried on in the name of Nationalism only; it was just as imperative that German Socialism should be represented. It was no mere coincidence that the cradle of National Socialism was in the heart of Bavaria, in Munich. It was symbolic that the German movement should arise in that same Bavaria that formerly, paying homage to separatist tendencies, had striven most to leave the union of the Reich.

It was symbolic that the German movement should arise in that same Bavaria that formerly, paying homage to separatist tendencies, had striven most to leave the union of the Reich. There it was that the young National Socialism had its first mission to fulfil, to bid defiance to those anti- German endeavours, and to make Bavaria itself the stronghold of the German idea.

Much has been written about the National Socialist programme, and still more has it been talked about. Distortions, misrepresentations, misunderstanding and the desire not to understand, have made the programme seem on the one hand thoroughly reactionary and on the other completely Bolshevist. But our programme has remained unchanged through all the storms and in the future, too, it will remain unchanged as the foundation stone of the new Reich.

One cannot in any way compare our programme with the programmes of the Middle Class parties. If one reads the countless party programmes which, in Germany more than anywhere else, have been drawn up in the last fifteen years, one sees over and over again that there is no trace of any moral or spiritual principle, even if in this or that sentence such things are mentioned to mislead the reader. In reality such party programmes simply represent the requirements of quite definite material interests. It may be that the Social Democratic programme represents the interests of a class of the proletariat, or that the Centre Party programme represents the interests of the universal Catholic Church, or again the many Middle Class parties emphasize, in some cases the interest of big industry, in others the interests of the small retailers or of agriculture or the processions. But in all cases these programmes represent pure materialism. In some cases one could see how certain parties drew up a new programme for each election and brazenly repudiated the old one. Sometimes the first half of the programme flatly contradicted the last half. The Centre at one election even went so far as to draw up two programmes, the one for the Middle Classes, the other for the workers. If any new political group was formed the essential thing was the programme. They talked boasting of their basic principles, whereas these were simply trivial embellishments, put on for tactical reasons in. the conflict of interests.

While we National Socialists always remained true to our basic ideas and never allowed anything to alter our principles, in tactics we were always willing to give way and to adapt ourselves to the particular situation. The reverse was the case with the other parties. They frequently stood firm as regards tactics, but were always ready to give up or alter their principles. It may be that, on very careful scrutiny, our programme seems, on this or that point, to be lacking in clarity. But one must on no account forget, that this is no political programme, cleverly thought out, discussed for months and prepared, and finally given a philosophical basis and baptized with scholars and politicians as its godparents. In the National Socialist programme a few men of the people without subtlety or cleverness have interpreted the deep longing of a nation which was already fighting for its rebirth in the midst of destruction, dissolution and collapse. The planks of our programme are fundamental principles and those maxims which are to guide our actions in the work of building up the new Germany. To take only one example : - It was laid down that War profits were to be taxed away. Immediately the clever ones rushed to the attack with the objection that today there are no more War profits. To be true this is no demand in the literal sense, but what it means is that the feeling of the people always rebels against the idea that individuals should be allowed to make a material profit out of the general distress. In the same way such a demand is directed especially against those who by exploiting the difficult position of the people sought to gain huge profits by the sale of war material, while the ordinary German was sacrificing his property, his family, even his life, without any thought of material gain, simply to serve his country.

The same protest would be made against those who, for instance, would seek to make a profit out of some natural catastrophe, while those who had been hit by the catastrophe were having to endure great hardship and misery. Broadly speaking it means nothing else than this - that the blood of the least of one's fellow-countrymen is worth more than all material profit. And so, as has been shown from this example, one could explain each maxim in a higher sense. If one looks at the programme in this way, as we instinctively feel it, one sees what great strength emanates from these maxims.

One understands also why it is that it is just the people which has felt the truth of our programme, that is to say of our principles, more deeply and clearly than it could understand the other programmes. Nevertheless with us the decisive thing was never the programme, that is to say, the paragraph, the dead letter. It was always the living meaning which gave us strength and enthusiasm for the mighty struggle. The Leader once said 'Germany has not collapsed from lack of programmes, but because there were too many programmes and too few men of action.' If programmes were the decisive thing, then the Democrats with the parliamentary parties would today be more firmly established on the throne than ever. How often have I been asked 'Yes, but what is actually your programme ?
And I could only point, full of pride, to our simple and gallant Storm Troopers and say : 'There stand the bearers of our programme. They bear it on their clear open faces and that programme is - Germany !' All principles which tend to further the recovery and the position of Germany we alone recognize as points in our programme; all other things which may be damaging to our country we condemn and they are to be destroyed.

The first few years seemed hardly promising for the new movement. It could only develop slowly and gradually. The party remained confined almost exclusively to Munich and the Bavarian highlands, and had gained a footing only in Nuremberg and Coburg. Hitler and his followers were laughed at, they were not taken seriously, until suddenly, at the end of 1922, a rapid advance took place. Already, when Hitler made a speech, the biggest halls were filled to the last seat. Audiences listened breathlessly to the new teaching and surrendered completely to the magic of Hitler's personality. But the party was still confined to Bavaria.

Hitler ruthlessly condemned the pernicious Marxist doctrines. With unshakable determination he and his men, and above all the small but confident detachments of Storm Troops, opposed the Reds everywhere. They went out into the poorest quarters of the towns, into the Red strongholds, right into Marxist meetings, and fearlessly disputed with Social Democrat politicians. It was first and foremost the war veterans and the rising generation who rallied to Hitler's standard.

The year 1923 brought the inflation and there with panic. In Bavaria at that time the Bavarian People's Party was in power, a Middle Class Centre Party, concerned solely in loosening the ties between Bavaria and the Reich. In Berlin, Social Democracy still reigned supreme. The Bavarian Government thought they could use the young National Socialist movement for their own ends and exploit its opposition to Red Berlin. They did not therefore resist the Hitlerite agitation. As the general ruin became daily more and more apparent, the Party became stronger and Hitler became more and more determined. The other patriotic societies had come progressively under his influence and leadership.

8. Black Friday - November 9, 1923

In Bavaria the Party had already reached its zenith. At the same time the Bavarian Government Party considered that the time had come to exploit the general discontent with the Berlin Government : they would move to the attack and therewith split the Reich.

Hitler himself was firmly resolved to prevent this happening and to use the disgust with Berlin to organize a united and general attack against the Government of the Reich as such. The events which led up to the so-called Hitler Putsch are well known and it would take up too much space to describe them here. On the 9th November, 1923, on the fifth anniversary of the shameful November revolt, it was planned to strike the decisive blow. Confidently trusting the solemn promises of von Kahr, Lossow and Seisser (Government, Army and Police), Hitler, in the night from the 8th to the 9th November, proclaimed the new Germany and declared the Government of the Reich to be removed from office. On the following day the march to Berlin was to have started. We know today that Herr von Kahr, as representing Catholic and Wittelsbach tendencies, had planned quite a different action for the 12th November. And so the movement, without knowing it, had, by its action, saved the unity of the Reich.

At about noon on the 9th November the first of the unarmed marching and singing columns of the fighters for freedom were treacherously shot down by the police near the Feldherrnhalle in Munich. Eighteen sacrificed their lives and many more were wounded.

Beside Hitler marched General Ludendorff, and beside Ludendorff myself as commanding officer of the Storm Troops. Hitler and Ludendorff were saved as by a miracle. I myself fell, seriously wounded by two shots. Abruptly and brutally the rattle of the machine-guns had wrecked the rejoicings and had murdered the hope of freedom. Once more, as has happened several times in German history, treachery prevented victory.

The young movement which had only just sprung up, seemed already destroyed. The followers were dispersed, the leaders in prison, wounded or in exile. To the weak, once more discouraged, it seemed as if Germany was now finally lost.

But it soon became clear that these sacrifices had not been in vain. The seed sown in blood began wonderfully to put out shoots. The fighters the activities, were united more firmly than ever. Hitler himself was stronger, more experienced, more confident in the future than ever before. During his imprisonment the situation seemed hopeless. But he had hardly been released when the enormous attractive force of this leader and prophet became apparent.

He took the banner into his own hands again, and immediately the old fighters gathered round him afresh and thousands of new ones as well.

The movement was now established not only in Bavaria, but also in North Germany. With the march to the Feldherrnhalle in Munich the young movement had made its entry into world history, and had taken over the leadership and direction of the struggle for freedom, honour, work and bread which was now beginning. For the future no other organization could lay claim to the same position. It was a Middle-class Government which had given the order to shoot down the soldiers of National Socialism at the Feldherrnhalle.

And therewith many honest German workers lost the last traces of mistrust towards the movement. The Middle Class parties could no longer take in the people with the lie that they represented the nation. At the Feldherrnhalle they had come out in their true colours, and there it was that National Socialism finally tore from the Bourgeoisie their distorted idea of Nationalism. In the same way the movement could no longer allow the Social Democrats to call themselves the representatives of Socialism.

The Middle Classes had taken the sublime conception of Nationalism, which is to promote the good of the whole people, and had degraded it to jingoism, which has its roots in alcohol and in the winning of profits.

In the same way the Social Democrats' had taken the pure conception of Socialism, which means service to the community and the right of each individual to live a decent life, and had degraded it to a mere question of food and wages.

Germany was split into two hostile camps; on the one hand the Proletariat, and on the other the Middle Classes.

The Middle Classes appeared as the representatives of Nationalism, hated by the workers as the symbol of compulsion and oppression; the Proletariat, hated and feared by the cowardly Bourgeoisie, appeared as the symbol of destruction and the abolition of private property. The two ideas seemed mutually exclusive and inevitably opposed to each other. If the one side seemed to offend against the nation, then the other side offended against the people. There could be no bridge built between the two parties; there could be no reconciliation. Hitler saw that the distortion of these two ideas had brought about the division of the people, and that as long as they remained distorted no unity was possible. Therefore he took the symbols from both parties and melted them in the crucible of our philosophy to make a new synthesis. The result was National Socialism, which is the unique and indissoluble union of the two ideas at their deepest and finest. He explained to the workers that there can be no socialism, no socialist justice, unless one is prepared to recognize the good of the whole nation. He who would better the lot of the individual must be ready to better the lot of the whole nation. At the same time he convinced supporters of the Middle Classes that they could never achieve national strength and unity unless they were ready to grant each individual fellow-countryman his rights, unless they were ready to look upon the lot of each individual fellow-countryman as their own personal concern. He explained to both sides that Nationalism and Socialism are not mutually exclusive, but are absolutely necessary to each other. He thus combined both ideas to one philosophy, and he had then logically to bring the representatives of the two ideas together and to unite them and thus achieve national solidarity. And so it will always remain Hitler's greatest merit that he did not bridge over the gulf between Proletariat and Bourgeoisie, but filled it in by hurling both Marxism and the Bourgeois parties into the abyss.

Thus the ruinous war between classes and parties was brought to an end, and the unity of the nation and the solidarity of the people was achieved.

9. The Tactics of Legality

But now the hardest and most difficult struggle began. The Party had to give up its revolutionary tactics and continue its advance by legal methods. Hitler did not want to expose his troops a second time to the hazards of a street battle; he did not want once more to provoke a collision between his followers and the armed forces. He knew that the armed forces, in so far as they were represented by the Reichswehr, were at heart on his side, necessarily on his side. He was himself too much a soldier; he loved this little German army too much to force upon it such a terrible conflict of loyalties. He knew, and had already said prophetically in his speech in his own defence in the Hitler trial at Munich, that the day would come when Reichswehr and National Socialists would stand together in the same ranks for the freedom of their country. Hitler was able to bring about this change of tactics : it was the 9th November, 1923, which made this possible, for no one could now accuse him of being too cowardly for revolutionary action. People could no longer say that he could only talk, but not act. He had proved that he could act. He had himself been at the head of his columns, and he and his subordinate officers had not on that occasion behaved like the Marxist and Communist demagogues, who stirred up their followers and sent them to the barricades, but themselves remained prudently in their editorial chairs and in their trade union offices and contented themselves with spilling ink while their followers spilled their own blood.

But this tactical change to the legal struggle did not at all mean renouncing the idea of revolution. In the Marxist vocabulary revolution means riots, street fighting, plundering of shops and houses, murder, arson, turmoil and disorder. But for National Socialists revolution is something great and mighty; it means the tearing away of what is old and rotten, and the breaking through of new forces which are strong and young. We carry out revolution continuously; each one of our meetings, each one of our newspapers, each one of our proclamations has been this higher kind of revolution. For we revolutionized the thoughts and feelings of the German; we fought, not for votes at an election, but for the soul of each individual. We wanted to make workers, peasants, shopkeepers and members of the learned professions, members of all classes, professions and churches, first and foremost Germans again. In hundreds of thousands of meetings we spoke in glowing words, we stirred up the minds of our hearers, we hammered into their brains and carved upon their hearts that there was only one thing which they must be 'Germans,' and that they had only one duty, 'Germany!'

These mass meetings were the sources of something quite unique. To begin with, we had meetings in smoky little inns or restaurants in the poorer quarters, in the midst of workers who had been roused to the highest pitch of hatred, and opposed to us were Marxist and Communist agitators. Very often such a meeting ended in a free fight, and there often were many wounded, and we were often driven and thrown out of the room by overwhelming odds.

But that did not prevent us from returning again and again with fresh courage; ever and again we stormed the Red strongholds and the number of our supporters grew. The workers had the opportunity to convince themselves where the truth lay, where loyalty to one's convictions gave strength, where leaders were brave and where cowardly. And then came men from all social strata and classes and from all professions and parties. The largest halls were no longer big enough; people stood in the street for hours before the beginning of a meeting when a prominent leader of the movement was going to speak. Their enthusiasm grew to ecstasy when the Leader himself made a speech. We were faced by indescribable rejoicing as well as whistling and disorder, unheard-of love as well as the deepest hatred, unique devotion and self-sacrifice as well as the crudest egoism and materialism. And so we went our way through the people, with complete confidence and with a clear aim before our eyes. We were outlawed and slandered, we had scorn and mockery poured upon us. We were the objects of an intense and indescribable campaign of hatred led by the newspapers which were in the hands of Jews.

Altogether the Jew had for long taken the lead in the fight against us. It was he who pulled the strings behind all our various opponents. At times he would appear as a reactionary, as a supporter of the German Nationalists, at times he was to be found as the soft and hypocritical and, on that account, craftier member of the Centre Party; and then again he would be the peaceful bourgeois of the People's Party. At other times he would look at us with the satiated middle-class face of a Marxist politician; and then again he would stare at us with the hate-distorted features of a Communist from the underworld.

However different the masks might be, the face behind was always the same - Ahasuerus, the Wandering Jew, always burrowing and agitating and considering every means legitimate.

The struggle was carried on with great anger and bitterness. On all sides the strength of our attack was noticed. The Roman Catholic clergy allied themselves with free-thinkers and atheists in the fight against us. There were continual underhand attacks on the part of the officials. We were outlaws; we were degraded to the rank of the second-class men; we had no rights and our Storm Troopers and Hitler Youth were free game for every Communist ruffian.

A bloody terror lodged in the streets of the big towns, a bitter struggle was carried on in the backyards and on the landings of the tenements in the poorest quarters of the great cities.

Our enemies always had the advantage of us in numbers and treacherously attacked and murdered our gallant men. It was mostly German workers who, as loyal Storm Troopers went to their death for their convictions and their country. The rage of the Social Democrats and Communists grew all the more intense when they were forced to see that the National Socialist movement did not consist of fine gentlemen retired officers, hysterical women and bourgeois profiteers, but that 70 per cent particularly of the Storm Troops, consisted of workers, manual workers who were then joined by brain workers. Without distinctions of birth or wealth or social class, officers stood in our ranks beside workers, peasants beside professors, all filled with the sacred idea, all loyal followers of the Leader. But now, too, it was first and foremost youth which flocked to our standard and the old who had remained young in their hearts.

It was once said that the future must belong to us, because we had youth on our side, but we could answer; 'No, youth comes to to us, because the future is with us.' It would take up too much space for me to describe further that wonderful time We had to suffer oppression from above (from the authorities), bloody terrorism from below (from the Communists), and social ostracism from the cowardly bourgeoisie. But all that only strengthened the movement.

When it was at last realized that our victorious progress could no longer be checked from without, the attempt was made to break up the movement from within, to undermine its strength. But though occasionally someone might take a false step, yet altogether these attempts broke completely on the firm wall of loyalty, love and trust.

10. The Leader

And then came the first election, and we sent twelve members to the Parliament of the Reich. We then had only one task, everywhere and at every time to attack. Like pike in the carp pool we worried the well-fed parliamentarians in their meditative repose. The first flourish of trumpets for the battle was sounded in the midst of those pleasant debates which were never meant seriously and between the flat, insipid and empty speeches. The parties became uneasy when a National Socialist member took his place at the Speaker's desk. The state of affairs was sharply criticized; the words fell on the backs of the guilty ones like lashes from a whip and the people were with us.

Our battle-cry - 'Germany awake !' - had stirred up the stragglers. The next election saw an amazing increase. From twelve members in the Reichstag we rose suddenly to 107. The world held its breath and listened. From now on other nations too began to reckon with the new movement. One could no longer speak of a sect, no longer call us sectarians or fanatics, and therewith consider the matter settled. To be true, we are fanatics, for nothing big can be achieved without fanaticism. Where would Christianity have been without its zealots ? Yes, we were white-hot with a fanatical love for our people. But we were fanatical too in our hatred of those who were destroying it. More and more did our names become known as the foremost fighters and loyal lieutenants of our Leader We ceased to be private individuals; home life, the family, all those things became of minor importance. From now on we belonged to the movement and therewith to our people and country. But before us all stood our Leader, Adolf Hitler.

At the present time there is probably no man on whom the attention of the whole world is concentrated so intensely as on the Leader. And yet there is no man whose unique quality is so difficult to describe. Everyone who knows the close inner bond between Hitler and his men will understand that for us followers it is axiomatic that the Leader must possess any quality attributed to him in its highest perfection. Just as the Roman Catholic considers the Pope infallible in all matters concerning religion and morals, so do we National Socialists believe with the same inner conviction that for us the Leader is in all political and other matters concerning the national and social interests of the people simply infallible. Wherein lies the secret of this enormous influence which he has on his followers ? Does it lie in his goodness as a man, in his strength of character or in his unique modesty ? Does it lie in his political genius, his gift of seeing what direction things are going to take, in his great bravery, or in his unbending loyalty to his followers ? I think that, whatever quality one may have in mind, one must nevertheless come to the conclusion that it is not the sum of all these virtues ; it is something mystical, inexpressible, almost incomprehensible which this unique man possesses, and he who cannot feel it instinctively will not be able to grasp it at all. For we love Adolf Hitler, because we believe deeply and unswervingly that God has sent him to us to save Germany.

And it is a blessing for Germany that in Hitler we have the rare combination of a keen logical thinker, a really profound philosopher and an iron-willed man of action, tenacious to the highest degree. How seldom are the gifts of genius combined with the will to action. In Hitler this synthesis is complete.

For more than a decade I have stood at his side, and every day I spend with him is a new and wonderful experience. From the first moment that I saw and heard him I belonged to him body and soul, and to many of my comrades the same thing has happened. I passionately pledged myself to his service and have followed him unswervingly. In the past months I have received many titles and honours, but no title or honour has so filled me with pride as the title which the German people have given me : 'The most loyal lieutenant of our Leader.'

These words express my relationship to my Leader. For more than a decade I have followed him with unbending loyalty, and with the same unquestioning loyalty I shall follow him to the end. But I know that towards me the Leader is filled with the same feeling of loyalty, and I know, and can proudly say, that I have the unqualified confidence of my Leader. This confidence is for me the basis of all my work.

So long as I stand firm in this confidence I do not mind what comes my way; nothing can touch me, neither overwork nor intrigues from within or attacks from without. But our opponents know that too, and that is why they agitate so wildly and shamelessly in this direction. One can read daily in some foreign newspaper that the quarrel between Göring and Hitler has become more acute, or else there are grotesque reports to the effect that Hitler wanted to have Göring arrested but the police refused to carry out the order for arrest, or else that Göring tried to overthrow Hitler but the attempt failed. The attempt is made to represent me as being filled with envy and suspicion and wishing to play the principal part, or it is said that the Leader would be jealous of any increase in my power. Anyone who is familiar with the situation in Germany knows that each of us possesses just as much power as the Leader wishes him to have. And no one has any real power or has any control over the executive of the State unless he is behind the Leader and has the Leader with him. But against the Leader's will, or even without his approval, he is completely powerless. It needs only a word from the Leader to remove anyone whom he wishes to have removed. His prestige and authority are boundless, but perhaps it is just because he has such power, because his authority is so great, that he makes so little use of it.

If Adolf Hitler has appointed anyone to an official position that man will not be dismissed unless he has been guilty of treachery or shown himself completely incompetent. In the most generous way the Leader has always forgiven the mistakes of his subordinates. How often has he smilingly passed over mistakes and when pressed nevertheless to dismiss whoever was responsible, has often answered 'Every man has his weak points and everyone makes mistakes, but before all, I value men who have the strength to act at all. They may make mistakes, they may act wrongly, but the essential thing is that they should be able to act at all.' Each individual follower has the wonderful feeling of security, that no intrigues, no gossip, no scandal can injure his reputation with the Leader. The pure character of Adolf Hitler is impervious to such talk; he simply does not hear it. Adolf Hitler is also so great that he could never be jealous of the ability and talents of his collaborators or of their prestige with the people.

On the contrary, he is always pleased anew when he has found a collaborator from whom he can expect exceptional achievements. It is one of his qualities as a leader that he knows how to put the right men in the right places. Hitler does not wish for any personal dictatorship. He does not want to be enthroned in lonely majesty above his collaborators; he does not want to be feared by them; he despises flatterers and place-seekers. Adolf Hitler's ideal, which he has often stated, has always been to have a band of capable and determined men at whose head there must necessarily be a leader. In this connection he often spoke of 'King Arthur's Round Table.' Adolf Hitler never needs to be elected as chairman, leader or president of a cabinet, commission or popular assembly. Wherever he is, he is the Leader; his authority is a matter of course; in a wonderful way he always manages to bind his men to him, whether they be Ministers or simple Storm Troopers. His unique personal charm holds everyone in its spell. He allows his collaborators the greatest freedom in their own spheres of work and duty. There they are completely independent, and if at any time he really has to intervene, if he wants something to be done differently, then he does it in such a way that the person concerned never feels offended; on the contrary, he feels even more closely bound to the Leader than before. The men who surround Hitler are fighters who have grown up in the struggle of the last fifteen years, steeled by all the hardships which they have had to suffer.

They are rough, blunt men, but they are complete in themselves, each one of them doing his utmost in his own sphere, each one of them filled with the sole aim of serving his country and his Leader. It may be that in particular questions there are different opinions, but as regards the great aim all are united, and here again it is above all the commanding personality of the Leader and the love for him which makes of all these men one mind and one will. It has always been Hitler's ambition carefully to seek out the best man for every important post ; nothing then pleases him more than the fact that he has not been disappointed in his choice.

So many Cabinet meetings now lie behind us, so much work has been done in them and so many vital laws have resulted from them, and it has always been a real joy to be a member of this Cabinet and to be permitted to work in it with the other Ministers. Here we do not indulge in speechmaking; the points of view of parties and particular interests are not expressed ; there is no conflict of irreconcilable opinions ; the welfare of the people comes before all. No member of the Cabinet will ever forget how the Leader always judged the political situation correctly, how his prophecies always came true, how convincingly he was able to sum up what was important and essential in the discussions. The meetings often lasted far into the night, but nevertheless the strenuous work held the interest of each one of us to the end and made it seem as if time had wings.

If one wished to make the attempt to describe Adolf Hitler, what sort of man he is, and how he works, one would have to write a whole book. The daily life of the Leader is something which is ever changing, ever new, ever stirring. Full of amazement, full of wonder and love, and filled with the most complete trust and confidence, the people sees its Leader grappling with this mighty burden of work. At every hour of the day and until far into the night his fellow-countrymen stand in front of the Chancellor's palace.

They are kept there by the consciousness that behind those walls and windows the Leader is working for the people, for them who stand outside and wait. Some mysterious spell holds them there as if rooted to the ground; and if they think they have caught, for even the fraction of a second, a glimpse of their beloved Leader at the window, then the storm of enthusiasm breaks. And thus it is all over Germany; wherever the Leader goes there is rejoicing, gigantic crowds; all want to be where he is, to see the Leader. One sees their eyes shine, particularly those of youth; one sees in their boundless gratitude crowds of men and women reach a state bordering on ecstasy; like an electric current the news passes through the teeming masses - 'The Leader is coming !' It is always the same - whether in the north, the south, the west or the east of Germany, in the town or in the country, whether he is speaking to students or leaders of industry, or whether he drives past the marching columns of the Reichswehr on manoeuvres, or whether he goes to the German workers in their factories - everywhere the spectacle is the same, everywhere the same feeling, everywhere this unique enthusiasm, which can come only from the most complete confidence, the most unquestioning belief, and the deepest gratitude. The German people know that they now have a leader again.

The German people are thankful that at last a man has grasped the reins with iron hands. The German people breathe again because at last a man is now thinking and working to abolish need and distress, and because they will no longer be forced to lead themselves. The great error of the previous system of liberalism was to imagine that the people wanted to govern themselves, to lead themselves. No, the people want to be led and to be governed; and, to be true, the people demand one thing, and that is that their leaders should be possessed with the sacred conviction that all their work and strength must be dedicated solely to the advantage and the good of the people. And the German people know that the longed-for and inspired leader is Adolf Hitler !

11. The Brüning Government

The year 1932 will always be considered as one of the most important turning-points in German history. And, in fact, it is a year full of the most thrilling events, of great tension, of mighty controversies. German life seemed to have reached its lowest point; everywhere things had come to a standstill. A veritable twilight of the gods seemed calamitously to have settled down on parliament and its parties; at last it began to be realized what was happening among the people; the party men woke up from their deep parliamentary sleep, disturbed by the hostile mutterings of an embittered people. Decisive political events followed one another rapidly. There was one election after another; the avalanche of meetings rolled over the country. On the one hand we had the National Socialists passionately attacking, stirring up and firing the masses; on the other hand the Communists passionately attacking too, and desperately resisting; the other parties of a Middle Class, red or black complexion, hopelessly trying to defend themselves. The gentlemen who were in the Government became afraid. But it is well known that fear makes people stupid, and that became apparent when one Government decree followed the other, each one being more stupid than the last. Once more they thought it would be possible to hold back the mighty millions of the National Socialist movement with ridiculous attempts at suppression. Behind the campaign against us were the Social Democrats, but in the vanguard were Middle Class politicians. Brüning and Groener were now the foremost fighters against the movement for freedom.

The monkish ascetic Brüning, a scholar out of touch with the world, but boundlessly conceited, and the democratic and feeble General Groener surpass one another in their hatred of National Socialism. Both were discontented politicians, whose petty ambitions had been disappointed, but who knew nothing of what the people needed, of the mighty drama in which they thought to play the leading part, but in which they were nothing but marionettes. We see a spectacle of the most shameful discord, but nevertheless, however strongly opposed the parties might be on the positive side, on the negative side they were firmly united by a paralysing fear of National Socialism. They might fight one another about officials' salaries, the raising of tariffs or taxes on dogs, but as soon as it was a question of keeping Hitler out of office they came together to form a single line of defence. And so the scenes change in this political theatre. Brüning Cabinet I falls, and after some weeks and with a few changes Brüning Cabinet II is presented to the German people. Which of those gentlemen at that time suspected the deep disappointment of the German people ? When the first Brüning Cabinet resigned the people were possessed with the single hope that now at last their champion, Hitler, would come to power. The hope was disappointed. But after no more than a few weeks the Brüning ship finally sank. Once more hope was revived; once more the couriers hurried between the President's palace, the Chancellor's palace and the Hotel Kaiserhof. I should like to draw attention to Dr. Dietrich's excellent book With Hitler to Power. (The Chancellor's palace was the negative pole and the Kaiserhof the positive pole in this political system of high tension.) On the 13th August, 1932, the tension was discharged, and the spark destroyed once more the hopes of millions of the best Germans. The torment, distress and shame were still not to end.

But the roll of thunder that followed this flash of lightning was even mightier than before. The foundations were shaken to the depths, and it was only the iron will of Adolf Hitler and his overwhelming authority that prevented the political tension from becoming the raging tempest of evil war. Hitler's hour seemed still not to have come. Today we know that the 13th August, 1932, had to be; today we are even thankful to Providence for this 13th August. For what would have happened if Hitler had accepted the conditions which were then presented to him and had entered the Papen Cabinet as Vice-Chancellor ? The idea of Hitler being Vice-Chancellor shows the complete lack of psychological understanding on the part of the then Government. The offer was purely and simply a political farce. One could offer Adolf Hitler anything; in view of his qualities he could be appointed to any post, but everywhere only as head, as the first man. The suffix 'Vice' or 'next in rank' before Hitler's name was a sheer impossibility and was felt by all his followers to be an insult. The man who alone had been chosen by fate to save Germany was now suddenly to accept a purely representative post in order, at the best, to go on fighting the usual day-today parliamentary battle and to defend the political aims of a Middle Class Government as its deputy. It is necessary at this point to examine the intentions of a Middle Class Government which was prepared to take Adolf Hitler into the Cabinet as Vice-Chancellor. By that offer they hoped to achieve two things : first, the embarrassing and powerful opposition of the National Socialists would be silenced; and, secondly, National Socialism would have been deprived of its political force; it would have lost its nimbus and gradually have been crushed in the parliamentary treadmill. Hitler, without himself being able to influence its policy, would have to have taken over the responsibility for the inaptitude and political weakness of every Middle Class Cabinet.

Catastrophe would soon have followed, for either the movement would have lost in strength or else he would have resigned again after a few weeks. But then the whole world, and all the political parties in Germany, would have rejoiced and declared 'So that is what the National Socialist leader is like. He accepted the responsibility of office only to show that Adolf Hitler was possible in sterile opposition, but impossible as a constructive statesman. Only a few weeks were necessary to show that National Socialism could not control the situation !' To this it will be objected that Hitler could have imposed his will on the Cabinet.

We know today that that would have been impossible, for Hitler would not have had the actual instruments of power in his hands. General Schleicher would have continued to lead the Reichswehr, a man who, during the whole of his political career, has done nothing else but try to torpedo and overthrow his predecessors. At heart a sworn enemy of National Socialism, he would have taken a special delight in destroying the movement in this way. The Prussian police, however, according to the same scheme, were to be put under Gregor Strasser. Herr Strasser, who at heart was just as much opposed to Adolf Hitler as Schleicher, as was shown a few months later, was resolved to work against Hitler and to attack Hitler. There remained the Storm Troops as an instrument of power. We know today that that Middle Class Cabinet would never have tolerated the slightest use of the Storm Troops as a political instrument of power. Anyone who saw the beginning of the Hitler Government, particularly in the Cabinets of the states, knows that here one would have come up against insurmountable opposition. In addition to this the parliamentary system was to have been allowed to continue; it was even proposed to go on governing in the regular parliamentary manner. For the Party, that would have meant death. The Party could well fight in opposition within the parliamentary system, but it would have been impossible for Adolf Hitler to govern in a democratic parliamentary way.

It was therefore completely obvious and absolutely necessary that Adolf Hitler would have to refuse. The tension among the people had greatly increased. Everyone longed to see Hitler at last in the Government. In our own ranks, too, there were those who were discouraged and thought that Hitler should have entered the Government all the same. These people thought that further suspense would be unbearable, that the Storm Troops could no longer stand further persecution, further terrorism and suppression. But the Leader knew better; he knew that the mood of the Storm Troops would always remain the same, always as resolute and unafraid as the mood of the Leader himself. He knew his Storm Troops better, and he, as master in the play of political forces, here, too, did the right thing. It must have been a wonderful encouragement to him to hear, as he drove through the crowds after the 13th August, 1932, ever and again the cry 'Stick to it, Leader; stick to it !' The people, with its sound instinct, had correctly grasped the situation. The people wanted to give its Leader all or nothing.

And so the struggle of the year 1932 continued, if possible with even greater bitterness and intensity. We had warned Chancellor von Papen, we had explained to him that we were compelled to attack him, not for personal reasons, but because of the post he wished to fill.

Again and again we explained to him that there was only one possible solution, and that was to make Hitler Chancellor. It would have been quite conceivable for Hitler to have been Chancellor and for there to have been no other National Socialists in the Cabinet. But it was quite unthinkable that there should be a whole Cabinet of National Socialists and the Chancellor not a National Socialist.

We proclaimed that anyone who stood between us and this goal of ours would be passionately attacked.

We proclaimed that anyone who thought to draw his sword against us would be ruthlessly pushed aside.

12. The Papen Government

And so at last the struggle against Papen began. From a personal point of view we were sorry, for we thought highly of him as a patriot and a man ; but politically the struggle was an unavoidable necessity. And so in the very first decisive meeting of the Reichstag we had at once a sharp encounter. That famous scene occurred in which Herr von Papen wished to dissolve the Reichstag, but I, as Speaker of this Reichstag, sought to prevent him doing so.

It was seemingly just playing with words a race with the second-hand of the watch, but in reality it meant that the National Socialists were steadfastly resolved to reach their goal. It was ultimately of no importance how and where he handed me the President's writ; what was important was that we resisted it with all our strength. Amidst the wild applause of our followers the Papen Cabinet retired and the Reichstag continued to sit. I knew that to go on sitting was only a pretence, but that, too, was unimportant. Here again what was decisive was that the conflict had taken place and the impossibility of continuing to play the parliamentary game was clearly demonstrated to the people. After a few months Papen fell, as had been foreseen. That had to be, for first of all he had then the whole National Socialist movement against him, and secondly he had the Minister for Defence, Schleicher, apparently on his side.
But any Chancellor who has Herr von Schleicher on his side must expect sooner or later to be sunk by the Schleicher torpedo. At that time there was a joke in political circles - 'General Schleicher ought really to have been an Admiral, for his military genius lies in shooting under water at his political friends !'

Once more the people were presented with the spectacle of a Government crisis and once more the tension grew to breaking-point. Once more we have the same manoeuvring between the Kaiserhof and the Wilhelmstrasse, the same hither and thither. Would Hitler be Chancellor or not ? Once more we see all those forces running together which were united in their uneasy consciences and in their fear of Hitler being appointed.
The ambitious General von Schleicher seemed at last to have reached the goal of his political career : 'Chancellor and Minister of Defence in one.'

The next step could then only be dictatorship and his own omnipotence. But now that the General could no longer be a wirepuller in the background, now that he had himself to stand in the dazzling limelight of publicity as leading character on the political stage and was himself pulled and pushed by countless conflicting forces, it became apparent that he was in no way fit for his post. He himself imagined perhaps that he was an astute politician, but nevertheless he did not understand in the least the feeling of the people. And that is the vast difference between all the leaders of post-war Germany and Hitler.

They all of them knew well their own parties, their clubs and associations, but they all of them more or less ignored the people; they did not take the people into consideration. Hitler, on the other hand, was the only one to stand with both feet among his people, and was therefore the only man entitled to represent this people.

13. The Schleicher Government

Of all the Chancellorships of post-war times one can well say that Schleicher's was the most pitiful. Schleicher hoped to keep himself in power, hoped to be able to govern, by playing off one side against the other, by promising every Party a great deal and not keeping any of his promises. The absurd idea of getting support for himself from the Marxist trade unions, which had already completely broken down, shows by itself this man's entire lack of political understanding. His idea of splitting the National Socialist party from within and of enticing away some of its subordinate leaders in order to checkmate Hitler shows the same lack of political understanding. Strasser, up till then one of the most powerful men in the movement, worked with Schleicher against the Leader, and in the middle of the fiercest battle, and five minutes from the goal, attacked his Leader from behind.

While the Leader was fighting Schleicher in this hard struggle and was holding with iron will and dogged determination to his demand for the Chancellorship, Strasser was negotiating with Schleicher behind Hitler's back in order to get a place in the Cabinet. It was Strasser who was seeking to win over other officers in the Party to his side in order to bring pressure to bear on the Leader and to force him to yield. These gentlemen had thought it all out so splendidly - Schleicher Chancellor and Minister for Defence, Strasser Prime Minister of Prussia and Vice-Chancellor. But Hitler was to be pensioned off and robbed of all power.

Hitler had strictly forbidden all his collaborators to carry on independent negotiations. I, who was then his political representative in Berlin, received my instructions daily drawn up beforehand in the most exact terms. Thus during the negotiations the Leader always held the reins firmly in his own hand. Now Strasser tried to get round this prohibition and therewith wantonly set fire to the solid structure of the National Socialist Party. The Movement can pardon everything except faithlessness towards the Leader; it never forgives disobedience, indiscipline or treachery. As soon as Schleicher's and Strasser's action became known a cry of rage went up. The other leaders, followers and supporters felt themselves more firmly bound to Adolf Hitler than ever before. Now more than ever all were determined to follow him blindly in iron discipline and to carry out all that he ordered. The negotiations were broken off. Schleichr was Chancellor, and therewith began the same passionate struggle as had been carried on against Papen. But for Schleicher we had not the personal sympathy that we had had for Papen. Schleicher had tried to bring disloyalty into the Movement in order to break it up. And that was not playing with one's cards on the table. For the third time the German people's hope that it would at last be saved was destroyed. One could hardly think that this extreme tension would pass off without an explosion. Pessimists declared that the Movement was now losing ground, that the Party could not stand this third disappointment of its hopes, and that supporters were beginning to drop off. Again Hitler was urged to give in. But now, too, in what was perhaps the most critical decision he had had to make, Hitler remained firm.

Above all the noise and chatter of the crowd his goal shone clear before him and, with prophetic gaze, he saw that his time was no longer distant. Here again we know today that we have to thank Providence that Hitler did not become Chancellor in those November and December days. For as things were then he would have had to have taken General von Schleicher as his Minister for Defence, and, since his treachery was not then known, Gregor Strasser would have been Minister of the Interior. Therewith both instruments of power would have been in the hands of men who at heart were out of sympathy with Hitler, and would in fact have rather seen him fall than prevail. Right from the beginning the Cabinet would not have been homogeneous; it would not have been able to work together harmoniously. That would necessarily have led to acute conflicts, and who can say what would have been their outcome?

And so this temptation passed too, but only because of the iron will and the wonderful political instinct of our Leader. The attacks continued. The masses participated perhaps more passionately than ever in the meetings and electoral battles; the Government was attacked still more hotly and ever and again they and their party confederates were driven into a corner. More and more did the people come to realize, and the old Field Marshal came to realize it too, that Schleicher's Government was incompetent and impossible. In addition to this, the President was disgusted with the way in which Schleicher had brought about Papen's fall and also with the way in which he was now governing. But Schleicher's sole political support was the confidence of the President. Only with the confidence of the President could he play his part; ever and again he was forced to borrow the authority of the venerable Field Marshal in order to fight his political battles. We all knew that if we could only enlighten the President and if he would then withdraw his confidence, Schleicher would be done for.

There would not have been one man, whether among the people or in the army, who would have been ready to fight for him. And so the year 1932 came to an end in such a turmoil of political passions as the German people had never before experienced. The suspense was almost unbearable and even more bitter conflicts were threatening, for the most difficult part of the winter was still to come. When the year 1932 came to an end Germany had reached the depths of suffering. The German people's time of trial had been marked by countless sufferings. The beginning of the coming year would either bring collapse or recovery. All the parties, all the leading politicians, all groups and associations had been tried. One had, so to speak, taken the last and the best horses from the stable and let them run. But they had all broken down. Men as well as parties, they had all failed.

14. The Victory - January 30, 1933

And so January 1933 began, the month which for long will be reckoned as perhaps the most memorable in German history. By the middle of the month it was already clear that the final decision was coming. There was feverish activity on all sides. From January 20th on I was, as political delegate, in constant touch with Herr von Papen, with Secretary-of-State Meissner, with the leader of the Steel Helmets, Seldte, and with the leader of the German Nationalists, Hugenberg, and was discussing with them future developments. It was clear that our goal could only be reached by the union of the National Socialists with all the remaining national forces under the sole leadership of Adolf Hitler. And then it was seen that Herr von Papen, against whom, for political reasons, we had once been forced to fight, now realized what a momentous occasion this was. With sincere cordiality he entered into alliance with us, and became the honest mediator between the aged Field Marshal and the young lance-corporal of the Great War. Without hesitation Seldte threw the Steel Helmets into the National Socialist scale and took up his stand loyally and firmly behind Adolf Hitler.

The agreement with the German Nationalists was more difficult, for there the remains of the Party system were too firmly lodged. It was clear, and in the first weeks I often said so to Hugenberg, that it was high time that the German Nationalist Party should dissolve itself in order to flow into the great river of National Socialism.

But at that time an agreement had to be come to, or everything would have been destroyed. The President was willing to appoint Adolf Hitler if the unity of the national forces would thereby be assured. The difficulty in coming to an agreement was due to the fact that on the one side stood the National Socialists, superior to all other Parties in numbers and above all in power, and on the other side stood the leaders of a Middle Class Party which, on account of its parliamentary past, demanded powers out of all proportion to its size or importance. The chief difficulty, however, was that Adolf Hitler demanded as a sine qua non that immediately after the formation of the Cabinet a general election should be held. The German Nationalists, on the other hand, passionately opposed this idea. They saw quite rightly that the wheel of history would pass over them, and they knew that the mighty forces of National Socialism would be doubled or trebled, particularly as they would have the additional nimbus of having seized power. But at last an agreement was reached.

On Saturday, the 28th January, 1933, I could report to the Leader that in its essentials the work was finished and that now at last one could count on his being appointed. But we had had such bitter disappointments in the past that we did not dare to speak about it or to mention it to even our closest friends. And so it came about that Adolf Hitler's appointment, which followed on the 30th January, 1933, surprised not only all the public, but the whole Party as well. Right up to the night from the 29th to the 30th one could still reckon with all kinds of intrigues on the part of the former Cabinet. For a moment it almost seemed as if Schleicher would not retire without putting up a fight, but he had already hopelessly lost the battle; everything was fixed. On Monday, the 30th January, at 11 o'clock in the morning, Adolf Hitler was appointed Chancellor by the President and seven minutes later the Cabinet was formed and the Ministers sworn in. Previously it had taken weeks, sometimes months, to form Cabinets; now everything was settled in a quarter of an hour. With the words of the aged Field Marshal : 'And now, gentlemen, forward with God !' the new Cabinet started on its work.

I had, as Hitler's representative, often in the past year gone backwards and forwards between the Kaiserhof and the Wilhelmstrasse, and I shall never forget the moment when I hurried out to my car and could be the first to tell the expectant crowds : 'Hitler has become Chancellor !' At first there was breathless silence, but then the crowds dispersed in wild haste. One saw boys, men, even women rushing away to spread the glad tidings, to tell others that Germany was saved. I cannot describe what our feelings were as we once more came together in the room at the Kaiserhof. How wonderfully had our luck changed at last and how wonderfully had the aged Field Marshal been used as an instrument in the hand of God. On the 13th August, 1932, and in November of the past year he had refused to appoint Hitler; but now, at the right and decisive moment, he had appointed him.

The first Cabinet meeting was fixed for five o'clock in the afternoon. We were all filled with a solemn feeling when, for the first time as Chancellor, Hitler addressed us and in wonderful words described our goal and the tasks which lay before us. But outside in the streets of the capital, and in all the towns of Germany and in all the villages, bells were ringing, men were rejoicing, were embracing each other, were happy in the intoxication of a great and noble enthusiasm.

Everywhere singing columns marched through the streets Suddenly the cry went up that in the evening there was to be a torchlight procession for Hitler and Hindenburg. With lightning speed the tidings spread. From all districts, from all the suburbs of Berlin, the crowds streamed in. Storm Troops, Guards (SS), Steel Helmets and patriotic associations assembled in close columns at the various meeting places, lit their torches, and then marched past the President's palace in such a procession of thanks as had never been seen before in the history of the capital. There, at the lighted window of the Palace, stood the aged and venerable Field Marshal and, deeply moved and filled with gladness, looked down upon a people that had become free and happy again. And a few houses further on there stood, motionless, the man who had earned the thanks of the whole people - the man who had never weakened in the bitter, unceasing struggle, who had always held the banner firmer when others faltered, who, through thick and thin, had always remained true to his people - the Leader of the German people, its Chancellor : Adolf Hitler.

> And that was the memorable night in which
> the new German freedom was born.

Soon after the seizure of power and during the elections of the 5th and 12th March, 1933, the revolution slowly, and without any visible stimulus from outside, grew stronger and stronger and prevailed. The Ministers who were not National Socialists had to realize, and have in fact realized, that they could achieve nothing with ordinary reforms, because a whole people was girding itself for action.

The people wanted at last some outward sign that it had become free and that a new age was dawning. The only outward symbol of this fight for freedom which the people knew was the Swastika flag.
It was therefore only logical that in the course of the revolution this battle standard should have been hoisted on all public buildings. The Field Marshal, being conscious of the vast significance of what had happened and desiring to show his recognition of the revolution, ordained that the Swastika, together with the black, white and red, should be the official flag of the Reich. We are deeply thankful to him for this wise decision.

Activity in all spheres was given a new direction. An important task for me was the reorganization and building up anew of the Prussian bureaucracy. And so the law was passed for the purging of the bureaucracy. This law gave me at last the power to remove all officials whose attitude or character made it unlikely that they could usefully collaborate in building up the new state. But it also gave me the power to purge the bureaucracy of the excessive influence exercised by the Jews.

15. My Task

The Leader appointed me a member of the new Cabinet. Before my appointment I had already been Speaker of the German Reichstag and I was to continue to hold this office. But the Leader gave me the Prussian Ministry of the Interior, above all things in order that I should overthrow and crush Communism in this, the greatest State of the Reich.

He wished me to root out this destructive and traitorous party, and to inspire the State officials with the austere philosophy of National Socialism in place of the existing corrupt Marxistbourgeois ideas. In Prussia at that time the Marxist Government under the Social Democrat Braun was, on paper and de jure, still in power, but de facto this Government had been deposed by the then Chancellor von Papen on the preceding 12th June and had no rights. Nevertheless they still, proud and undaunted, called themselves the 'sovereign' Government of Prussia and therewith proclaimed right up to the end the full absurdity of their existence.

And so I became Commissioner for the Interior in Prussia and at the same time Minister of the Reich. An enormous task lay before me. The Prussian Ministry of the Interior has always been one of the most powerful of the Reich and State Ministries. It was here that Severing and Grzesinski had played their political game. It was from here that they had carried on their terrorist activities against the National Socialists.

It was for that reason that every National Socialist, and above all the simple Storm Troopers, felt particularly proud and gratified when this Ministry was put into the hands of an old champion of the movement. For it was from here that they had been persecuted and tormented, and from here all those orders and decrees had been issued to suppress them; here it was that the directions had been given for the brutal persecution of the fighters for freedom.

And now, on the 1st February, 1933, amidst the deafening applause of a crowd of several thousands, the victorious swastika was hoisted to the main flagstaff, before a guard of honour consisting of police, guards and Steel Helmets and a band playing the Prussian ceremonial march.

(a) The Reorganization of the Police

I had taken on a heavy responsibility, and a vast field of work lay before me. It was clear that I should be able to make little use of the administrative system as it then was. I should have to make great changes. To begin with, it seemed to me of the first importance to get the weapon of the criminal and political police firmly into my own hands. Here it was that I made the first sweeping changes of personnel. Out of 32 police chiefs I removed 22. Hundreds of inspectors and thousands of police sergeants followed in the course of the next month. New men were brought in, and in every case these men came from the great reservoir of the Storm Troops and Guards. My task was to inspire the police with an entirely new spirit.
Previously the Police had been degraded to the role of whipping-boy for the Republic, partly by compelling them to belabour the Republic's opponents and partly by always shifting the responsibility on to the shoulders of minor officials, the leaders being too cowardly to stand up for their subordinates. Now that was all going to be changed. Authority would be in the right place.
After a few weeks one could already notice how the bearing of the Police had changed, how they had become more assured and self-confident, how the embittered officials gradually became valuable officers and police-sergeants. They in no way received military training, but were nevertheless imbued with the traditional soldierly virtues. Devotion to duty; loyalty and obedience were demanded of them, and above all that they should pledge themselves unreservedly to serve the National Socialist State and the new Germany. Young and tried officers who in the past years had not allowed themselves to be cowed by the Republic were promoted and put into responsible Positions. A particular troop, Police Division Wecke, was picked out and equipped with all weapons allowed to the Police and formed the vanguard of the new Police force. But thereby the ambition of other squads was aroused, and they strove to show that they could be just as good and efficient as these picked men. As an outward sign of this newly-awakened feeling of pride, I forbade all officers and inspectors, and later on all other Police officials, to carry batons. It was not in harmony with my feelings

as an officer that the Police should run round and strike at the public with batons. A Police officer only resorts to force in cases of extreme necessity, only when it is a matter of life or death, but then he must draw his revolver and shoot to protect State and people. But up to then the state of things had been such, that when some policeman fired his revolver in selfdefence he became involved in criminal proceedings which usually resulted in his being embittered and punished. No wonder then that the Police no longer dared to act in a brave and resolute way, but only worked off their rage with their batons where they could safely do so.

The police of the Severing regime knew perfectly well that our men were unarmed and could not shoot at them; they therefore dared to belabour them with their batons. But they proceeded against the Communists in quite a different way. They knew that the Communists might shoot at them with revolvers; that they had often experienced, and officers and men had often been shot. But nothing was done by the Government to protect them. The Communists, the 'political children' of Herr Severing, were always defended in the end by their Red sympathizers. Now everything was fundamentally changed.

I gave strict orders and demanded that the police should devote all their energies to the ruthless extermination of subversive elements. In one of my first big meetings in Dortmund I declared that for the future there would only be one man who would bear the responsibility in Prussia, and that one man was myself. Whoever did his duty in the service of the State, whoever obeyed my orders, and took severe measures against the State's enemies, whoever ruthlessly made use of his revolver when attacked, could be certain of protection. Whoever on the other hand was a coward and avoided a fight and looked the other way, whoever hesitated to make use of his weapons, would have to count on being thrown out by me at the earliest possible moment. I declared then, before thousands of my fellow-countrymen, that every bullet fired from the barrel of a police pistol was my bullet. If you call that murder, then I am the murderer. Everything has been ordered by me; I stand for it and shall not be afraid to take the responsibility upon myself. Whoever sees the Prussian police of today, after three-quarters of a year, will be quite unable to recognize in them the police of Herr Severing. The core of the police force was excellent, and what we have succeeded in doing in the last few months has been to make of the Prussian police an instrument which gives the State the right feeling of security and gives the police themselves the proud feeling that they are the first and sharpest weapon of the State. By the changing of the ugly uniform and the awarding of flags to squads, the self-respect of officers and men was increased. The new oath of allegiance now had a deeper meaning and to fulfil it had become their sacred duty.

(b) The Organization of the State Secret Police

The state of things in the political police was very bad indeed. Here I found nearly everywhere trusted agents of the Social Democrats, the creatures of Herr Severing. These men formed the ill-famed 1 A division (political police). I could in the prevailing state of things make no use of them. To be true, the worst elements had been removed by my predecessor, Bracht. But now I had to make a complete job of it, and for weeks I was personally engaged in the work of reorganization.
Finally I alone created, on my own initiative, the 'State Secret Police Department.' This is the instrument which is so much feared by the enemies of the State, and which is chiefly responsible for the fact that in Germany and Prussia today there is no question of a Marxist or Communist danger. Without taking seniority into consideration, I put the ablest men I had into this 'State Secret Police Department,' and put it under the command of the most capable of my younger officials. Every day I am further strengthened in my opinion that I chose the right men. The achievements of Diels and his men will always remain one of the glories of the first year of German recovery. I was also Most actively supported by the Guards and Storm Troops. Without their help and support I should never have mastered the enemies of the State so quickly and effectively. I have now reorganized the Seeret Police once more and placed it under my direct control. By means of a network of centres in the provinces, with Berlin as the headquarters, I am kept daily, I might almost

say hourly, informed of everything which happens in the vast Prussian State. The last refuge of the Communists is known to us. However often they change their tactics and change the names of their couriers, a few days later they are tracked down, reported, watched and arrested. We had to proceed against these enemies of the State with complete ruthlessness. It must not be forgotten that at the moment of our taking over the Government there were, according to the March election figures, about fourteen million supporters of Communism and Marxism.

These people were indeed not all of them enemies of the State. The greater part of them, countless millions, were good Germans, led astray by insane theories and by the emptiness and spinelessness of the Middle Class Parties. It was therefore all the more urgent that these people should be rescued from error and brought back once more into the community of the German people. But it was also just as necessary to take strong action against the deceivers, agitators and chiefs themselves. And so the concentration camps were set up, to which we had sent first of all thousands of officials of the Communist and Socialist Democratic parties. It was only natural that in the beginning excesses were committed.

It was natural that here and there beatings took place ; there were some cases of brutality. But if we consider the greatness of the occasion and all that had preceded it, we must admit that this German revolution for freedom was one of the most bloodless and most disciplined of all revolutions in history.

(c) The wiping out of Marxism and Communism

Certain unpleasant and undesired phenomena are the concomitants of every revolution. But if, as in this case, they are so few, and if the aim of the revolution is so completely attained, nobody has any right to work up an agitation about them.

But I most strongly protest against the flood of mean and dastardly calumnies and atrocity stories which have been spread abroad by creatures who have fled from Germany and have no honour and no Fatherland. By spreading these stories, the Jews of Germany have proved more conclusively than we could do in our speeches and attacks how right we were in our defensive action against them. Here the Jew is in his element, lying and concocting atrocity stories, from a safe distance throwing buckets full of mud at the people and country whose hospitality he had enjoyed for decades. The decent Jews have only the members of their own race to thank that they are now treated all alike. They can send their protests to the Jewish organizations abroad which play the chief part in the atrocity campaign. Our case against the Jews is not merely that the part they played in every profession was out of all proportion to their total numbers; it is not merely that they had made themselves masters of finance, capital; it is not merely that they carried on usury and corruption on a vast scale and that they exploited Germany and sucked the blood from her veins; it is not merely that they were primarily to blame for the crime of the inflation, that they pitilessly strangled their economically weaker German hosts.

Our chief accusation against the Jews is that it was they who provided the Marxists and Communists with their leaders, and it was they who occupied the editorial offices of those subversive and defamatory newspapers which besmirched with their venom and hatred all that to us Germans was sacred; they it was who cynically distorted and ridiculed the words 'German' and 'National,' and the ideas of honour and freedom, marriage and loyalty. No wonder, then, that the German people was at last seized with a righteous anger and was at last unwilling to allow these parasites and oppressors to play the part of master any longer.Only he who has observed the activities of the Jews in Germany, only he who knows the Jew from his behaviour in Germany, can fully understand the necessity of what has now been done.

The Jewish question has not yet been completely solved. All that has happened up to the present has simply been defence of the people, a reaction against the ruin and corruption produced by Jewish race. If we look at it from this point of view, we see that the revolution was perfectly ordered and bloodless. It destroyed what was old and rotten, and brought to the front what was new and undefiled.

The Secret Police have contributed much to the success of this revolution and have helped to defend its achievements.

In the midst of this constructive work the great fire broke out which burned the cupola and chamber of the Reichstag. Criminals had planned this fire, had set fire to the German Reichstag in order to give the already moribund Communist Party the signal for a last desperate attack before the Hitler Government was firmly in the saddle. The fire was to be the signal for a general reign of terror on the part of the Communists, for a general rising and civil war. It is not because of the noble motives of the Communists that those results did not take place ; they did not take place simply and solely because of the iron will and the strong arm of Adolf Hitler and his fellow-fighters, who struck quicker than the enemy had calculated and harder than they could suspect, and, at the first blow, crushed them once and for all.

In that night, when I had given the order for the arrest of 4,000 Communist officials, I knew that before the dawn the Communists would have lost a great battle. But now our task was to inform the people of the terrible danger that had threatened it. At last it was possible to obtain an insight into the Communists' most secret plans and their organizations and aims. We could see now what criminal and ruthless means these inhuman creatures intended to use in order to destroy a brave people and a proud empire. I have been reproached with publishing old instructions as the Communist orders for civil war. Does anyone really think that an order is less dangerous because it was issued years before ? Does anyone really think that we must judge the Reichstag fire more leniently because we can say that it liad already been planned by the Communists several years before ? Today when I am asked by bourgeois politicians if this extreme defensive action was really necessary, the Communist danger really so very great, if I did not go too far - I can only reply with amazement and contempt : 'Yes, if you Middle Class cowards have no more Communist danger to fear and have escaped the horrors of a Communist revolution, it is not because you, and people like you, existed, but because, while you were talking away at your dilettante parlour

Bolshevism, there were men who saw the danger for what it was and removed it.' If I am further accused of having myself set fire to the Reichstag in order to get the Communists into my hands, I can only say that the idea is ridiculous and grotesque. I did not need any special event to enable me to proceed against the Communists. The record of their crimes was already so long and their offence so atrocious that 1 was in any case resolved to use all the powers at my disposal in order ruthlessly to wipe out this plague. The firing of the Reichstag did not, as a matter of fact, at all fit in with my plans, as I have already pointed out in my evidence at the Reichstag fire trial. It forced me to act sooner than I had intended and to strike before I had finished making the necessary preparations. For me there is no doubt whatever that those who instigated and planned the fire were the Communist Party, and that there must have been several persons who actually did the deed. The one who was caught was probably the clumsiest and stupidest of them. But the incendiaries themselves were not ultimately responsible. Their spiritual fathers and the secret wire-pullers behind the scenes are the real criminals against the German people and the destroyers of German culture.

(d) Prime Minister of Prussia

It very soon became clear to me that it was absolutely necessary that I should, besides being Prussian Minister of the Interior, also be Prime Minister. Only if I held this post could I properly carry out my task of exterminating subversive ideas, doing away with the Middle Class Parties and bringing in the new order. For this reason I settled the ridiculous question of the 'sovereign' Prussian Government. I also got Herr von Papen, as had been previously arranged, to retire from his post of Commissioner for Prussia in order that the Leader could give the post to me. It was only because I was able to strengthen the position of the Prussian Ministry of the Interior through the authority of the Prussian Prime Ministership that it was possible for me to carry out all the necessary reforms. For the post of Prussian Prime Minister was now more important and stronger than before. In the preceding years he had merely been a parliamentary figure and had not

been able to do more than influence the general direction of policy, but now the post meant unrestricted authority. The Prussian Prime Minister was now responsible for the whole of the Prussian State, particularly now that the Chancellor, after the Statthalter Law was passed, had transferred his rights as Statthalter of Prussia to me.
During my stay in Rome at Easter a particularly gratifying telegram from the Leader informed me of my appointment as Prussian Prime Minister :

'I appoint you Prime Minister of Prussia as from today (10th April). Please take over your duties in Berlin on April 20th.'

'I am happy to be able to give you this token of my confidence in you and gratitude for the great services you have rendered to the German people during the ten years in which you have been a fighter in our Movement for the regeneration of Germany. I thank you, too, for your services as Commissioner for Internal Affairs in Prussia in successfully carrying through the National Revolution, and above all I thank you for the unique loyalty with which you have bound your fate to mine.'

Since my appointment, which was thus the result of Hitler's confidence in me, I had the fate of Prussia in my hands and was conscious of being able to take part, from the Most important position in the Reich, in Adolf Hitler's great work of reconstruction. For Prussia has had at all times a mission and responsibility beyond her own borders and that has been 'The solution of the German Question.' Laws passed in Prussia often served as a pattern for the other States by virtue of the newly-created sovereignty of the Reich and its Chancellor. For this reason I tried as soon as possible to put our National Socialist principles into practice in Prussia. This was made possible through the creation of a totalitarian State, that is by the victory all over Germany of the National Socialist Party and its continuance as the sole political organization in the country. It was also made possible by the Leader giving me full authority. I joyfully undertook the mighty task of turning a Prussia which had become rotten through Marxist misgovernment into a new State inspired with the spirit of Frederick the Great. The Diet

was immediately abolished. In its place I put the Prussian Council of State. This Council of State consisted of men who had been appointed by me partly on account of their high position in the Party or in the Storm Troops, and partly because they had distinguished themselves in other ways.
Their task was to help me with their advice, to study drafts of laws, to make suggestions, and to keep up the living connection between Government and people. But the Council of State only has an advisory capacity. It can make no decisions, neither can it take over any responsibility. The Prime Minister alone carries the responsibility and no committee can relieve him of it.
The principle of leadership was hence introduced in its purest form, at the same time maintaining a living contact with the people.

Our task was everywhere to build up anew, and we can proudly say that we have accomplished a great work.

During the first weeks I sat night after night until 2, 3 or 4 o'clock in my office in the Prussian Ministry of the Interior. Later on I moved over to the Prussian Ministry of State. Special departments were put under my direct supervision, such as the State and Municipal theatres, which were all threatened with complete ruin and had to be entirely reorganized. This was a task which demanded strong nerves and a great deal of time. I had always been very interested in forestry, and now I was supervisor of the greatest forest estate in Germany, namely the Prussian State forests. Here, too, I wished to set out in an entirely new direction. I therefore put this department, too, under my direct supervision and created the necessary foundations and passed the necessary laws.

It was indeed a full and active life into which the Leader had called me. I was President of the Reichstag, Prussian Prime Minister, Prussian Minister of the Interior, and in addition a firm National Socialist who continued to hold public meetings in order never to lose contact with the people.
The tasks were often overwhelming, but on the other hand they steeled one's strength and spurred one on to achieve one's utmost.

But over everything there was the blessed feeling of happiness that one was permitted to serve one's country in one of the most important positions, and to be supported by the wonderful confidence of the Leader and - this perhaps for a man the most splendid of all - to be able to form and to create.

(e) Aviation

As a former airman - I was given yet another sphere of work. The Chancellor had rightly seen that the civil air lines were of great importance. They had therefore to be taken out of the control of the Ministry of Transport. A new Air Ministry was formed and the Leader appointed me as its head. He gave me the task of making the German air service the best and safest in the world and of raising the commercial air fleet to a new pinnacle of importance. Above all, the German flying spirit, which had been held down by the chains of the Treaty of Versailles, was to find a new outlet in air sports.

There was not much in the way of machines for me to take over. They were mostly old models, for there were only a very few up-to-date passenger planes. Here, too, I had to give my whole strength to the great task.

It also seemed to me absolutely necessary to convince the other Powers that Germany too had at least the right to a defensive fleet. Germany, surrounded by Powers bristling with armaments and herself completely unarmed, does not possess even a single chaser machine or a single observation plane. She is completely at the mercy of other Powers. It is true that Germany has been permitted to keep a small navy and a small force for land defence. But what is the use of this horizontal defence if an enemy plans to attack us vertically ? Not a single French soldier, not a single enemy battleship, need advance against Germany; without any risk to themselves the air fleets of France, Poland, Belgium, Czechoslovakia and other countries could fly over Germany and wipe out thriving German towns and villages, and kill and mutilate innocent men. Who can here speak of equality of rights ? And what trace is there here of the right to defend oneself ?

And where is there any trace of the much talked about international morality and international spirit and of European civilization ? Never and at no stage of the negotiations did we ask for offensive planes or bombing planes. We only wanted to defend ourselves, to have defensive machines against enemy attacks, to have chaser machines against enemy bombing squadrons. Why are we not allowed such machines ? If the other powers say they never wish to attack, if they have no evil designs on Germany, why should they not permit Germany to defend herself ? Why may Germany not possess antiaircraft guns ?

The suspicion is indeed forced upon one that it is intended at the appointed time to fall upon Germany and to invade her in all safety from the air. The world must at last awaken to the fact, and the nations be made to realize, that to grant Germany a small army and navy for her security is a mere mockery so long as the vertical line is undefended and open to all attacks. It is therefore my task to go on exhorting and demanding until Germany has at last obtained true equality and security.

16. The Making of a Nation

For ten months Hitler has ruled Germany. How short the time, but how great the achievement ! How much has happened ! In a few months we have succeeded in doing what we thought would take years. In all spheres an advance has begun. Everywhere we have moved forward. The German peasant, up to a few months ago without rights and liable at any time to be turned out of house and farm, now stands fast once more on his hereditary land. His land is no longer a commodity; it has been removed from the clutches of speculative usurers and has again become sacred and inviolate. We are in the midst of a mighty campaign against unemployment. Nearly seven million unemployed looked expectantly and with despairing eyes to Adolf Hitler.

Today, after ten months, nearly half of them have work and maintenance. That is indeed an unprecedented and unheard-of achievement on the part of Adolf Hitler. Public confidence has been awakened and this leads to a further rise in employment. This is, however, also actively stimulated by schemes on the part of the Government. Thousands of kilometres of great new roads for motor traffic have been planned and work on them has already begun; new canals are to be made, the motor tax has been abolished, insurance premiums lowered, thousands and thousands of new cars are daily being built. Part of the rates has usefully been applied to schemes for creating work. The completely corrupt and almost bankrupt Old Age Pensions scheme has been abolished by a boldly conceived law which at the same time saved the members' contributions. Theatres, films, music and the Press have been freed from the Jewish spirit and purified of all subversive influences. A new blossoming has begun in all branches of cultural life. Movement and State have become one in a common National Socialist philosophy. The Party and the Storm Troops are closely bound up with the Government and assure thus a continuous and undisturbed development.

But the most important thing, the greatest and most wonderful of ideas, has become a reality : Hitler has achieved what seemed impossible. Out of the division and disunion of the German people, out of all its parties and classes he has made one united people. What had previously in German history been at the most a dream has now become concrete reality. Out of forty-two million voters forty million have formed themselves into one single front, a wonderful event, a glorious harvest from the seed sown by Adolf Hitler. The 12th of November, 1933, will remain for all times the most glorious day in German history.

A little time ago Hitler spoke the following unforgettable words : 'The 12th November has not only shown that forty million Germans are one with the Government; has not only shown that the overwhelming majority of Germans supports the policy of the Government; the 12th November has above all shown that Germany has again become decent and honourable !' The 12th November has shown that Hitler was right when he said again and again : ' The core of the people is healthy. I believe in my people, and this people will one day show the world that it has taken thought and risen again !' The 12th November vindicated Adolf Hitler's faith in his German people.

The hopeless weakness and impotence of the Reich in foreign affairs was the inevitable result of the preceding system's catastrophic internal policy. Here it was seen that the foreign policy of a people is always the result of its internal policy. Internal policy remains of primary importance. For it is impossible to deprive a people from within of all its national virtues and allow it to become demoralized and cowardly and at the same time to act in a heroic way towards foreign countries. It was through treachery that the Republic had come into being. It was only logical that it should be carried on by treachery and by abandoning the nation's vital rights. And nevertheless the previous system was especially proud of its foreign policy and its successes in that sphere. It was pointed out that Hitler had in a few weeks undone all those successes, and in the shortest possible time had left behind nothing but wreckage in the field of foreign policy. Those who made such statements were already inwardly exulting when in the first months of the year the ring about Germany became closer and closer. They pointed out that Hitler had made enemies of all nations, but they omitted to say that during the whole of the last decade those nations had shown nothing but hostility towards Germany. The iron ring had always been there, but the previous system had succeeded in deceiving their own people and getting them to believe that other nations were filled with goodwill towards Germany. Such goodwill had - in reality - never existed. Germany had been nothing but the whipping-boy of the other nations at Geneva. International agreements were made at Germany's expense. The smallest of South American States did not play such a pitiful role at Geneva as the so-called Great Power, Germany. It is true that when Hitler took over the government it seemed as if suddenly all the hostile forces had joined together to bring about Germany's fall in the field of foreign policy. The émigrés played their part with their vile campaign of calumny. Former leaders of the Social Democrats appealed abroad for armed intervention in Germany. At last they removed their masks, and the German worker could now see what scoundrels - and the word is far too weak - had ruled his destiny during the past decade. Forgetting their country, they were so infamous as to prefer to see Germany go up in smoke and flames in a French and Polish invasion rather than be driven from their own lucrative posts.

An unparalleled campaign of hatred, supported by lying Press reports, brought feelings in the countries round Germany to the boiling-point. Germany now suddenly appeared as the disturber of European peace; Germany, who was completely unarmed and struggling with her own grievous need, was now said to be threatening the world and to be a danger to France, to a France armed as no nation in the history of the world has been armed. And it seemed as if people believed these assertions.

17. For Equal Rights, Honour and Peace

But then Adolf Hitler showed that he was not only the re-awakener of Germany at home, but, as he now demonstrated to the world for the first time, in foreign politics also a statesman of the highest rank. Into the midst of this tense atmosphere he hurled his famous peace speech before the Reichstag. The world waited feverishly on that afternoon for what the new German Chancellor, the much abused man, the wild militarist, would now have to say. And he spoke of the German people's deep desire for peace, of its terrible poverty and distress; he spoke of how it needed all its forces to come out of this distress. He spoke, too, of his fight against subversive influences and against unemployment, and solemnly declared before the whole world that nobody in Germany and no German statesman thought of attacking any other country, and that the new Germany wanted to co-operate with her neighbours in a spirit of sincere mutual esteem.
But he spoke, too, with deep earnestness and glowing eloquence of the reawakened German feeling of honour, of Germany's desire to be master of her destiny. He pointed out also that we had made great sacrifices to the cause of European peace and were willing to make still further sacrifices, but that there was one thing that could never be abandoned, one thing that even the most cowardly could never yield, the one thing that for a people, if it would be free, was more vitally necessary than air - the nation's honour.

Our enemies were disappointed and filled with rage that in a few hours this masterly speech had torn to bits their whole network of lies. But in other countries those men sighed with relief who really wished for peace, and therefore understood that one could not require of a great people like the Germans what one would oneself feel to be unbearable. The threatening thunderstorm seemed to have passed. But the enemies of Germany went on working feverishly in order to increase to an immeasurable extent Germany's difficulties in the League of Nations and to plunge the German people into grievous conflicts. In the Disarmament Conference responsibility had been shifted on to the wrong shoulders. The disarmament of the highly armed States was no longer discussed. The proposals in this direction were hardly worth serious consideration.

Here, too, the discussions were concerned solely with Germany. The disarmed and, from a military point of view, weakest country, was to be still further disarmed. Germany was again to be stamped before the world as the disturber of European peace. Shameful conditions were to be imposed on Germany in order to humiliate the Hitler regime before its own people and before the world. The politicians at Geneva were superior in cunning to our negotiators. They cleverly managed always to present Germany as being obstinate and unyielding. Suddenly in bombastic, hypocritical words they declared that the equality, to be true only a theoretical equality, which had been promised to a Schleicher Germany in December could not apply to a Hitler Germany.

One could now clearly see what they were aiming at. We Germans now knew what would happen at the Disarmament Conference at Geneva. There was only one thing now at stake and which could not be the subject of bargaining. This was our honour and the question of our equality among the nations. After fully considering the matter and carefully examining his own conscience, Hitler did the one thing possible. He took the bold step of checkmating the League of Nations and its intrigues in one move by declaring that Germany would withdraw from the Conference and the League. Once more the Press answered this bold and skilful move with a howl of rage.

How could Hitler permit himself to escape from the net which had been laid, and how could Germany dare to break the traditional and popular rules of the Geneva game in which Germany had always to be the loser ! At last the League of Nations was forced to realize that it was up against a first-class opponent.

But Hitler had freed himself from oppressive and unbearable fetters. Germany, for fifteen years bound and impotent in foreign politics, had at last regained her freedom of action. For the first time Germany was not merely the anvil; for the first time the hammer blows of an active German foreign policy sounded. By joining the Four Power Pact, the brilliant conception of that really great statesman, Mussolini, Germany had shown that she was ready to associate herself with any conference or political action which seemed honestly to serve the cause of peace.

Simultaneously with her departure from Geneva the last election campaign began in Germany. This election was not, like the previous ones, a struggle between innumerable fronts. A united nation was defending itself as one man; it was demanding as one man that it should be granted equal rights, and was fighting as one man for its honour against those countries that were hostile to Germany. The German people showed the world that it was desirous of collaborating with all its strength in any policy that would really serve the peace of the world. But, on the other hand, it also showed the world that if it wished to negotiate with Germany it must grant this Germany the same respect, the same rights and honour, that other nations would demand for themselves. The German people, almost to the last man and the last woman, supported their leader and his policy of freedom and honour. Germany has also in the future no desire to rob or humiliate any other nation, but this same Germany will not allow any nation to rob or humiliate her.

May the other peoples realize that the Leader in Germany is the first guarantor of European peace. For the task which Hitler has taken over, and the fight which he is waging at home, does not only concern Germany. Hitler's mission is of importance for the history of the whole world, because he took up a war to the death against Communism and therewith raised a bulwark for the other European nations. Many times before in world history have mighty spiritual struggles been decided on German territory. It is our solemn belief that if, in the mighty struggle between Communism and National Socialism, the former had won, then the deadly bacillus would have spread from Communist Germany to the other European countries. The day will come when the other countries will begin to realize this, and on that day France, England and other peoples will be thankful that at the critical moment there was an Adolf Hitler in Germany.

The great struggle on the outcome of which the future not only of Germany, but of Europe and the whole world, depended was the struggle between the Swastika and

Soviet Star. If the Soviet Star had been victorious, Germany would have perished in a bloody Communist reign of terror, and the whole of the western world would have followed Germany into the abyss. The victory of the Swastika has at any rate averted this terrible danger, and for that we must give thanks to God.

Once more it has become possible for Germany to rise again and for us to create a healthy Germany. But Germany is, and will remain, the heart of Europe, and Europe can only be healthy and live in peace when its heart is healthy and intact. The German people has arisen and Germany will again be healthy. For that we have the guarantor who is Adolf Hitler, the Chancellor of the German people and the protector of their honour and freedom.

Hermann and Edda Göring

For more informations :

Balder Exlibris
www.balderexlibris.com

Viva Europa
www.vivaeuropa.info

Aldebaran Video
www.aldebaranvideo.tv

The Savoisien
www.the-savoisien.com

Free PDF
www.freepdf.info

PDF Archive
www.pdfarchive.info

Aryana Libris
www.aryanalibris.com

Histoire Ebook
www.histoireebook.com

Hermann Göring during First World War

LENCULUS
Exegi monumentum aere perennius

Reichsmarschall Hermann Wilhelm Göring

www.ingramcontent.com/pod-product-compliance
Lightning Source LLC
LaVergne TN
LVHW091603060526
838200LV00036B/975